Memoirs of an Old Dyke

Memoirs of an Old Dyke

Jinx Beers

iUniverse, Inc.
NewYork Bloomington

Memoirs of an Old Dyke

iUniverse books may be ordered through booksellers or by contacting:

iUniverse
1663 Liberty Drive
Bloomington, IN 47403
www.iuniverse.com
1-800-Authors (1-800-288-4677)

ISBN: 978-0-595-52624-6 (pbk)
ISBN: 978-0-595-62676-2 (ebk)

Printed in the United States of America

iUniverse Rev. 10/17/08

DEDICATION

This manuscript is dedicated to the
June L. Mazer Lesbian Archives
and the women whose personal efforts
keep the Mazer active and prominent
in preserving the history of our
lesbian community for
future generations.

TABLE OF CONTENTS

Part 4

Life Post the Military

Part 5

The Lesbian News Story

Part 6

Activities and Observations

Part 7

The Later Years

ACKNOWLEDGMENTS

Special thanks to
Wendy Averill and Marilee France.

Without their support, love,
and encouragement
this manuscript would never
have been completed.

Additional thanks to
Linda Shinn
for her comments, as well as reading
and editing expertise.

FORWARD

As I write this memoir I have no idea what will ever be done with it, if anything. I'm not writing in any particular order, either within or between categories, however I have ordered the sections in what I considered a logical manner. The "chapters" definitely overlap. I don't do this to confuse the reader, but to allow myself the freedom to write what pops into my mind at the moment.

I started writing about my memories when I was in my early sixties and have spent several years on it, taking time out in the middle to flirt with death. As I finish the manuscript I'm approaching my seventy-fifth birthday. For all practical purposes the story is complete, although I reserve the right to add anything new that might happen in the future up to my death, and I give permission to anyone who wishes to add a prologue concerning my demise.

Why have I written my memoir? Maybe I wrote it for my own ego or a justification of having lived. Or perhaps there is someone out there who is interested in reading about an old dyke who has been out of her personal closet since 1955 when she was twenty-two years old, well over fifty years ago. It was an astounding and difficult time, before there was a "gay and lesbian movement."

I don't claim to be a particularly exceptional person or lesbian. Indeed, I think I was pretty run-of-the-mill for a time filled with emerging lesbian heroines. Still, I did participate in the gay/lesbian movement of the 1970s and '80s, called "the second wave" by historian Barbara Love. The real beginning of the movement is left to history, like Sappho, Gertrude Stein, and Ann Bannon to name but a few from different eras who I consider more important.

As each generation before me, I've been written off by the generation that came after me. That's OK, because much of what I and hundreds of lesbians of my age accomplished laid the base for what followed. If, as you read this, you have the freedom to be yourself wherever and whenever you wish, it is because the lesbians who came before you opened doors so you could step through without harm, physically or emotionally. I have seen lesbians come from not being able to walk down the street without being stopped by the police, to lesbians who've won the right to marry in some states. It took women seventy years to win the right to vote and lesbians and gays have won the right to marry in less than half the time!

Although I participated in several aspects of the lesbian/gay movement in Los Angeles, my biggest achievement was founding *The Lesbian News*. Born in controversy within our community, it was a major undertaking for which I'm very proud. I cannot tell you how many lesbians have thanked me and assured me the LN assisted them in their coming out process and in finding others of their sexual orientation. I have been given several awards for my work with the LN, including being named a "Feminist Who Changed America." However the most important item I received was an unsigned postcard that simply said, "Thank you for being there." I framed it, put it on my wall and have cherished it for over twenty five years.

You can find my story of founding *The Lesbian News*, which has now existed for more than thirty years, elsewhere in this manuscript. So, too, you can find memories of my childhood, recollections of my time in the military, my general life experiences as an adult, and some activities in the community as well as personal observations and opinions.

If indeed you are reading this memoir, I want you to understand this is not an exhausting autobiography (much of which would be terribly boring), but memories I hope will give you some insight to who I am as a life-long lesbian, one who believes I was a lesbian in the womb.

What's In A Name?

I guess I should get the story of my name out there right off the bat. Yes, Jinx Beers is my legal name, and no, I wasn't born with it.

You need to understand that for more than fifty years I've refused to tell anyone what my first name was. It's not that there was anything wrong with the name; I've known women with the same name who were wonderful and the name fit them perfectly. It just never fit me. Besides there's more to the story than that when your mother wouldn't even call you by your first name!

I was the fifth of five children. My mother told me later in life she was determined I wasn't going to be named after any relative as the other four had been. She said she asked my dad to give her a list of names he liked. She named me Clara Jean Beers, and said Clara was the *best* of the names my dad had listed, but she got to pick the middle name. However, no one ever called me Clara. I grew up being called Jean and consider it a perfectly good name.

My sister Virginia was nine years older than me (and the next one up in age). When she was teaching Sunday School at about seventeen, and I was eight, she and I used to write poems for her young students. Just to lend a bit of mystery to the poems we would sign them "Ginnie and her jinx." Soon she began to call me "her Jinx," eventually dropped the "her," and I became Jinx to her. To my parents I was still Jean.

The year I was born must have been a good year for the name Jean. Because, a few years after my sister began to call me Jinx, I entered a health education class in high school and found there were five students in the class named Jean. That was it, I permanently became Jinx. Even as a teenager I didn't want to be like everyone else.

When I was eighteen I joined the Air Force, but of course they wouldn't let me join under my taken name. For four years I went through my regular service under my legal name, but everyone called me Jinx. After I was discharged, I decided to go to court and make Jinx legal. I was in the Air Force Reserve at that time and a young, inexperience attorney in my reserve unit said he'd represent me for a very reasonable fee. He also advised me that if I ever intended to own property, I should do the name change first to eliminate future problems.

On the designated day we entered a courtroom of people and families wanting to change their names. We didn't rate a judge; we were assigned a commissioner authorized to do this minor kind of legal stuff. First he spent a half hour wasting time asking each attorney how much time he needed, and chastising any attorney who said he needed more than a couple of minutes. Each case was then called individually.

First up was a family consisting of husband, wife and small child who wanted to change their last name from Rosenberg to Rose. The commissioner asked the husband why he wanted to change his name, and was told, "For business purposes." The commissioner spent the next ten minutes chastising Mr. Rosenberg for wanting to change "a perfectly good name." By law all you have to do is swear you're not taking a new name for fraudulent purposes. The commissioner, still fuming, had no choice but to grant the name change request. This should have been a warning to me.

Eventually my case came up before the commissioner, and my attorney and I stepped up to the bench. The commissioner read my petition and said: "You want to change your *first* name from Clara Jean to Jinx?" He looked up at me, apparently unhappy, and said in a very loud voice,"Is this a joke? Are you trying to be funny in my courtroom?" I answered no, it wasn't a joke. He chastised *me* for a while and finally went through the process of making me swear I wasn't changing my name for fraudulent purposes, and granted my petition.

One of the problems about having an inexperienced attorney is he wasn't able to think quickly. He stood there with his mouth open and said nothing. He never said a word until we were out of the courthouse. I'd like to think he was at least a little embarrassed about not speaking up for my petition before the commissioner.

It took my father many years to call me Jinx. Not because he objected, but because he wouldn't remember I'd changed my name. In the next few years he would be proud of himself when he remembered to call me Jinx. The rest of my family took to it pretty quickly.

There is one interesting aspect about being named Jinx, and that's the reaction of other people upon first being introduced. Over the years I've realized I get one of two distinct responses. About twenty-five percent do a double take and make some comment about my "being a jinx." That is, they view the name in a negative way. But three-quarters of the people I meet react in a positive manner, commenting the name is "cute," or "unusual." Since I received the name Jinx in a positive way, I think of it positively, and assume those who do not simply view life in the negative. That's their problem, not mine.

Throughout the world there are duplicate names in every language. How many Mary Smiths? How many Sean O'Connors? How many Mohammad Amirs? I don't know, but I'd bet you no where in this world is there another person named Jinx Beers!

A Note About Other Names

As to the names of the people mentioned in my memoir, in most cases the names I use are real, but limited to first names. Only those in my very closest circle would be able to recognize them. The few times I've used actual names are incidences that are public record, not just my recollection.

I have no intention of hurting anyone's feelings. However in a couple of vignettes I do write about behavior that might be embarrassing, albeit truthful. My intent is to write about myself and how the relationship affected me. But, for example, how am I going to explain how living with an alcoholic enlightened me without saying she had a drinking problem? In this case I don't even use a first name.

I have attempted to be circumspect when writing about others and included only the history required to speak about myself. If I failed in this effort at all, I apologize in advance.

PART 1

A FAMILY AFFAIR

1

Bits and Pieces of the Very Early Years

Born in the worst part of the Great Depression on Columbus Day, October 12, 1933 about 5:25 pm at the Women's Hospital on North Fair Oaks Avenue in Pasadena, California, it became clear to me at an early age I was a mistake. My parents had two boys followed by two girls in the first six years of their marriage. My mother was seventeen when she wed, but she had finished high school. Nine years after her fourth child, I arrived at a most inopportune time. My mother was thirty-two.

My older sister, Anne, who was eleven years my senior took care of me most of the time. Later in our lives we frequently talked about the fact that she raised me more than my mom, until she went off after WWII and got married. Consequently, it's no surprise that of all my family I grew closer to her than anyone else.

Anne turned out to be significantly taller and larger than I was, and until her passing at age eighty, she called me her "baby sister." She was a serious and dedicated person. Her husband contracted multiple sclerosis in his midtwenties, slowly deteriorating over the next forty years. Anne's dedication to taking care of him was astronomical in my opinion. Despite his personal dislike of me, my sister never suggested I wasn't welcome in her home. Not only did she take care of me when I was little, but protected me from knowing about the "unspoken" actions of my family until I was in my mid-thirties. Only once in eighty years did she pull back from me, but that was because she didn't like the person I was living with, and had little, or nothing, to do with me personally. Until her death I considered her a "port in the storm" if I ever needed one.

I actually have few memories before age six, except a few disconnected flashes. I remember being on welfare for a while and watching boxes of food staples being delivered to the kitchen and my mother being embarrassed, but accepting it. I want to remember riding on the back of our Shepard dog, King, who was very patient with me (I must have been very young for him to withstand my weight), but I suspect I'm "remembering" only because I was told it happened. We lived in Temple City during at that time. Do I remember riding my tricycle at about age three? No, I think that is only a memory of a picture. There was also a picture of me with King in the back of a stake truck, but I don't think I remember the actual event.

I do have distinct memories of living across from a dairy and alongside the Southern Pacific railroad tracks in El Monte. I would stand on our front porch and wave to the engineers as they went by. Most would wave back. There was a period where I would write down the engine numbers and knew about when each engine was due. For the rest of my life I've had a high interest in trains and model railroading, but not particularly in cows (although I love the cow ads for California cheese).

At that same residence there was an old silo and one of my brothers, Roy, would sleep there. One night there was a storm and the silo split open and fell down. My brother was totally uninjured; the silo had fallen out away from where he was sleeping. Also there, my mother would buy goat's milk from the landlady. The goat ate whatever weeds she could find. The milk tasted just awful, but I was forced to drink it anyway.

Then there was the first day of a new school when we moved to Monrovia. It must have been kindergarten. I cried and cried and cried because I had left my lunch at home. Finally the teacher gave in and let me go back home for it and return to school. I was fine from then on.

When we moved back to Pasadena I was six years old and it was there I had my first "romance" with Gwendolyn, the little girl who lived across the street. We used to play "house," and of course I was always the man-of-the-house and a doll was our child.

Most people have many memories going much farther back than I do. Mine are very limited. I believe I've blocked out that time because of a traumatic experience concerning my brother Roy when I was six.

2

My Non-Existing Brother

They tell me I once had a brother named Roy. Actually, his name was Lawrence Clifford, but after his birth certificate was signed, my father decided he was going to be named Roy. Too late officially, but it's what he was called for the rest of his life.

Which wasn't all that long.

Roy committed suicide when he was nineteen..

My sister Anne told me that Roy and I were buddies. When he was home, he would play with me, carry me around on his shoulders and generally make it obvious he loved me. I was six when he died; he was thirteen years older.

I know he existed because I have one picture of him, taken not too long before he died, sitting on a rock and holding a snake strung between his hands. However, I have absolutely no memory of *him*, only his funeral.

He committed suicide by jumping off the bridge into the Devil's Gate Dam in Pasadena. Back in those days there actually was water in the dam. Apparently he didn't know how to swim (neither do I). His car was found along the highway and his jacket was floating on the water. A couple of days later his body surfaced.

Suposedly he commited suicide over being rejected by a girl, Bonnie, who he had been dating. But I suspect there had to be more to it than that. Even a nineteen year old should know there are other girls and other romances to come. Roy had not been living at home for some time. He had gone to stay with one of my uncles in Oregon, but had returned for a visit. I have never been told why he left home so young, but I can understand why he might not want to stay there. It took fifty years for me to find out my older brother hated my father; maybe Roy hated our dad, too.

I remember Roy's funeral and everyone crying. I remember some of the flowers being carried home and put on our front porch. And I remember my father never spoke of him again. Neither did my mother, nor my sisters or brother Bill. I suspect that was by order of my father. But I do not remember to this day the brother I'm told I adored.

But there is an interesting side to this to which I have no answer. From the time I can remember I have loved reptiles. As kids we nearly always had desert tortoises, sort of an inheritance of our family. I actually had one tortoise for nearly thirty years before passing the 75-year-old guy on to a young neighbor who promised to take care of him. Since Desert Tortoises can live well over a hundred years, for all I know he passed it on to his child at some point.

But my love has always been snakes. I've caught them (when I was younger and didn't know any better), bought them (when I was younger and didn't know any better), and caught and released them (when I finally grew smart enough to understand nature needs to be left alone to raise her own). I've had king snakes, pythons, boas, water snakes, rattlesnakes, a very poisonous African Gabon, garter snakes, and many others. I've been bitten, (but never by a poisonous snake), constricted, raised mice to feed them, saved one snake's life, killed one accidently, and had the fascinating pleasure of watching a hog-nose snake I came across on a country lane in Tennessee go through his "dying" routine right in front of me, and then get up and crawl away as if he'd never seen me.

At one point I had a collection of about fifteen snakes in my apartment. Yes, in cages. Except for the one who escaped his cage and hid in the apartment for two months. I was really hoping he hadn't gone down one of the pool table pockets! Eventually we found him under the kitchen sink when he shed his skin around the mop bucket.

Now, where in the world did I get a love of snakes? Maybe from Roy, of whom I have the only photo that exists of him–a picture holding a snake. But I can't remember *him?*

3

The Skeleton In the Closet

One year when I was young my mother took me and my two teenage sisters to a cabin up at Big Bear Lake. We spent what my memory says was a couple of months up there. Although I can't remember the exact time of year, there wasn't any snow on the ground. Vacations were not a way of life in my family. Hardly anything pleasurable sneaks into my memories. I remember a day at the beach when I lost my pail off the pier and a young boy dove into the water and retrieved it for me, but going to the beach was a rare occurrence. Once in a while there was a Sunday afternoon drive, but gasoline cost money even then, and there was little money to spare. Besides, my father worked six days a week; he rested on Sunday or worked in his own yard.

My family did not eat in restaurants. A few times in my childhood my mother would sit us down at the Kress's lunch counter when we were out shopping. And once I and five other class mates were invited to celebrate a school mate's birthday at a Chinese restaurant in China Town. This was in elementary school before I became as sullen as I was as a teenager. I didn't learn about such foods as french fries, bagels, cheese cake, and other "exotic" morsels until I left home.

I don't believe my father ever saw a movie in his life. And my mother never went to the theater for a play until I was an adult and she was in her sixties and I and my partner took her to The Music Center to experience her first live performance. She loved it. During the war years I did see a few Saturday afternoon movies because we could get in by donating an old thick 33 1/3 record for the war effort. No money for popcorn.

You could say I lived a poor childhood, and you'd be right. So how in the world was it that we were vacationing in the mountains? And for two months, no less!

I actually didn't get the answer to that question for about thirty years.

Occasionally between about ten years old and thirty-something, I would get hints there were things in my past I didn't know about. I thought I got along well with my father. But once in a while my mother would hint that "if you only knew about your father" I wouldn't like him as well. Nice mom, huh?

As I became an adult, off to the military and back, off to work, off to college, I began to realize there was a skeleton in the closet that wasn't being spoken about.

Finally in my mid-thirties, my sister Anne told me what no one had wanted me to know about my father. That he had molested both of my sisters when they were teenagers. That period when we were living in the mountains was when my father was in jail. My mother had, after many years, turned him in to the police.

Much fell into place for me, particularly the questions my mother would ask me when I came home from working with dad (a gardner) in the summer. Questions I never understood at the time. She was trying to find out if he ever touched me. In fact he never did. He never made any kind of a move toward me that could have been misinterpreted.

I have a very good friend of many, many years who believes my father did molest me and I have simply repressed it like I blocked out the death of my brother. But I don't believe that because of two pieces of evidence. First, I have very clear memories since my brother's death, and none of them include any misbehavior, or suggestion of same, from my father. Second, when I joined the Air Force and took my physical, the doctor and nurse kidded me about being a virgin. My hymen was intact.

Although my sisters and brother never forgave my father and were bitter toward him until his death at age 93, I believe he had learned his lesson when he was sent to jail, and I was spared that indignity.

4

Mama, Dear Mama

While I was growing up I always thought I hated my mother. As an adult I came to realize I didn't exactly hate her, but I had little or no respect for her.

She was born in Vermont and brought up on a dairy farm in northern New York, just short of the Canadian border. She would tell stories about how poor they were. For Christmas she and her siblings would each get a stocking filled with nuts, candy and a small toy or two, and it was exciting for them. She had fond memories of the first sap running on the maple trees. There would still be snow on the ground and they would take a horse-pulled sleigh out, tap a tree and get a small container of raw maple syrup. On the way back to the farm house they would find a clean patch of unmarked snow and scoop up a couple of buckets. The snow would be packed tightly in a cup or glass and put outside to freeze. The maple sap was cooked a bit, and then poured over the iced snow. *Voila!* An early snow cone. This was her rememberance of fun and pleasure. The rest of the time she worked in the dairy or went to school.

When my mother was fifteen the family moved to Pasadena, California where she actually finished high school. She worked part time cleaning for my father's parents, which is how they met. At seventeen she and my father were married and she had her first child. I have the feeling she never had much of a childhood nor any freedom.

Somewhere along the line in the earlier years of their marriage, after two or three of the five children had arrived, my father's invalid mother moved in with them and mom had to take care of her as well as the children. Not much was ever told to me about that period, but I got the impression mom was not a happy camper.

By the time I was old enough to be cognizant of what was going on around me, my mother had fallen into a non-cooperative attitude. She loved to read and would spend most of her day doing so, much of the time in a rocking chair on the front porch. No matter there were dirty dishes in the sink, or the house needed cleaning, or there was laundry to do. Frequently dishes had to be washed in order to have enough clean ones to set the table for dinner. My father worked six days a week as a gardner, leaving the house soon after sunrise and returning at sunset, long work days in the summer. He wanted his dinner as soon as he got home, but my mother never closed her book to start dinner until she heard his truck in the driveway. My sisters were off on their own during the day and I was in school, but when we got home, we washed dishes and helped with dinner as we could.

I rarely brought any friends to my house as it was shabby and dirty. Rugs and furniture was always pretty well worn out in my memory. My home did not compare to the homes of my friends when I visited them. Even if they were as poor as we were, there was never dirty dishes in the sink or dirt on the floor. And I didn't have a concept at five, six, seven, eight that I should be doing something about it all.

From a very early age, however, I was conscious that I didn't want to be like my mother. And I don't believe I am except in physical attributes. My mom was overweight, as was her mother, her father, my older brother, my older sister and her daughters. After my mid-forties I began to put on weight and am now overweight myself. Genes will out, I guess, whether you want them to or not.

5

Family and Lesbianism

I've mentioned before, I had two older sisters. Anne was eleven years older and practically raised me, as my mother couldn't be bothered most of the time when I was very young. Virginia is nine years older and is the sister I wrote poetry with for her Sunday school kids. They reacted very differently to the eventual knowledge of my being a lesbian.

Maybe it was because Anne raised me she was mostly positive about my life choices. Among all the women I've lived with, and she never really knew about all the one-night stands and/or very short romances, she only disliked one that I'm aware of. Unfortunately, a rift occurred between Anne and myself over a family Christmas dinner held at her house. Most of the time we held family dinners at my mom and dad's, and my parents always went with the flow. Whoever I was living with at the time was always welcome in mom's house. My dad just never paid any attention.

This particular family dinner was held at Anne's house and, as my mother put it, Anne got to make the rules. Very simply, my partner wasn't invited. My mom went so far as to point out to me that if the dinner was being held at her house, of course my partner would be welcome, but she had no control over invitations to Anne's house. I made it very clear in return that if my partner wasn't welcome, I wouldn't be there. And I wasn't. Nor did my sister and I speak to each other for the next five years, long after that partner had left me. It was the principle of the thing.

Eventually Anne and I reunited and she accepted, and in some cases really liked, the women I was with. We never spoke of the estranged time between us, as if it had never happened, and went through the rest of our years together on extremely loving terms. She passed in her eightieth year after several years of heart problems, including wearing a pacemaker the last six. She had two girls, born fifteen years apart, with which I have a friendly relationship, despite their father's distrust of my being a lesbian. I suppose he had the antiquated concept of many fathers that I might seduce his children.

My sister Virginia and I have had a very up and down relationship. When she was in her late teens she converted to the Seventh Day Adventist religion, which was the faith of the parents of her deceased husband. She had lost her husband in a car accident and, of course, grieved with his parents, which brought them very close together. Not long after they all moved to Arkansas, and eventually Tennessee, where she has remained since. She married a farmer in Tennessee with four boy children and succeeded in giving him four more sons.

Virginia was very influenced by her religion and has been deeply religious since her conversion. Therefore, when my partner and I visited her home in Tennessee and I told her I was a lesbian, she became very conflicted. Her first reaction was, "Now I have another sister." But soon after we got back home I received a letter all but condemning me for my sexual orientation. She must have been thinking about it after we left, and did the flip-flop pretty quickly.

Over the next twenty five years or so, she alternated between writing me to tell me how much she loved me, and praying for my soul. I suppose there's no conflict in those two, but I felt as if she put me on an emotional see-saw. Gradually I came to realize she and I had grown so far apart we really had nothing to say to each other, or at least I had nothing to say to her. I've seen her only four times in the last fifty years and don't expect to ever see her again. She is now in her eighties and past traveling; I'm in my seventies and way past wanting to go visit her.

Interestingly, however, about ten years ago she started sending me needlepoint cards she had done herself. First for my birthday, then my birthday and Christmas. She needlepoints very well. Although the designs are fairly simple, they're her own creations. Not knowing what to do with them, I threw the first couple away. Then I realized they were works of art. I now have a collection including Valentine's Day, Saint Patrick's Day, Easter and Halloween, as well as several with Christmas designs and many wishing me happy birthday.

When she does write a note, I read much less about religion and nothing more about saving my soul, although she does tell me she loves me and thinks of me. As I write this, we are the only two left of the five siblings. Maybe she's thinking more of her own mortality.

I never knew Virginia's step children and only met her four boys when the were very young, except for one. I have a nephew who lives in Southern California and who keeps in touch. When he received a note from me letting him know my last relationship had ended after more than twenty three years, he was at my doorstep the next day, literally, to see if I needed any help. I've met his wife and kids and communicate by telephone or e-mail a few times a year or so. He appears to have no problem with my being a lesbian.

As to the males in my immediate family, my brother Roy died when I was six, so my being a lesbian never came up. My brother Bill and I never talked about it, but whenever I visited, he accepted whoever I brought along without question and always treated them kindly. I don't believe my father ever thought of it or anyone ever enlightened him, and he never questioned who I brought with me to visit.

That leaves my mother, who, between my returning from the Air Force at twenty-two and gaining the ripe old age of thirty-two, every so often would ask me when I was going to get married. I was not afraid to tell her. I was a open lesbian and figured she should be getting some clue from the women I brought to dinner and I kept looking for the perfect moment to bring my sexual orientation into a conversation. One day when we were talking on the telephone, it happened. She asked about marriage and I told her never, as I was a lesbian. There was a pause on the other end and my mother said, "Oh, I never thought of that." I told her to feel free to ask any questions if she wanted, but she never did.

So there you have it, fairly diversified reactions from members of my family regarding my being a lesbian, but mostly positive or neutral. All in all I think I've been quite lucky, particularly compared to stories I've heard from friends and lovers. It's quite possible my being a "tom boy" from a very young age helped to delineate the mind-set that I would be a lesbian in my adulthood. That might be stretching it a bit as I doubt there was a member of my family who knew what a lesbian was, except in theory, until I came along.

I don't *know*, as in truth, but I *believe* I was a lesbian from conception. Upon retrospect, my earliest actions and reactions point in that direction. I always resented males, not from penis envy, but from privilege envy. I always was strong both physically and temperamentally. I was sexually active from very early years. I never believed I was destined to be a wife or mother or hand-maiden to any male, although I have tended to melt under the glance of a female or two. I was recently asked when I came out, meaning out of my lesbian closet. My answer was that I never came out, because I never was in.

I wish every young lesbian had a family as accepting, if not understanding, as mine was. And I wish every family could embrace their lesbian members as unique and loving individuals. It would be a better world for all

6

My Other Brother

My oldest brother, Bill, left home when he was a teenager and joined the California Conservation Corps. He never finished high school. He joined the Army in WWII and was sent to Panama. He traveled through Tampa, Florida, met a 16 year old girl, married her in a week or so and shipped out. We knew he was in Panama because, unlike most young men, he liked to read, and we just happen to have a book on Panama. Of course during the War soldiers couldn't write home and tell anyone where they were. Had to keep military movements secret even if enemy spies knew their destinations before they did. Bill simply wrote home and referenced "that little red book on the second shelf." It didn't mean a thing to the military censors, but told us where he was.

Meanwhile his new wife, Alice, quit school and everyone stood around waiting to see if she was pregnant. She wasn't.

Eventually the war was over, Bill was discharged in Florida, began his marriage, got a job, and had a son in about a year. Then, a year or so after that, he decided to come back to California with his family.

Bill had been a trouble-maker in school, didn't get along with dad, and joining the CCC was a way to get away from home. He was fourteen years older than me, so I was only three when he left. I remember him dropping in a time or two in uniform before he left for Florida, but I never really knew him. Then suddenly, when I was fifteen, my brother Bill with wife and child in tow, moved back into my home, and took over. He joined my father in the gardening business and bossed everyone around as if he knew it all. I went from not knowing my older brother to hating him in a flash of time.

The next two years were miserable for me. I was constantly angry at him. I spent a lot of time up in my favorite tree, and as much time as possible away from the house. I also became angry at my parents, particularly my father because he let Bill take over. We're dealing here with the first-born and last-born competing for attention. With me being a teenager and him being nearly thirty, there was no contest.

Eventually he moved away from Pasadena, taking a job as manager of a grape ranch in Napa (in California, everything is a "ranch"). It wasn't until I became an adult that we finally became friendly and the anger subsided.

And I will give him credit for one thing: I only visited the ranch every few years, but when I did, I'd take a different woman with me each time. He always rolled with it. He always acted a gentleman with them. But never once in our interactions did he ever ask me any questions. I'm sure he realized I was a lesbian, but we never discussed it

7

My Only High School Friend

I had a friend in high school. Yes, I said that correctly. I had one person in my life I could really call a friend during that period of my life. The funny thing is, I have no idea why she was my friend.

I've mentioned before that I come from a poor family. My father worked hard as a gardener, but his was the only income for five people, my parents and three children since my brothers had left not too long after I was born. Since I have no memory of living with either of my brothers until after WWII, I can't count them in my early life memories. Gardeners didn't earn very much money.

First and foremost the rent and utilities had to be paid, and secondly food was needed. Meals were pretty simple: a lot of potatoes and bread. Standard Saturday night fare was macaroni and hamburger with sauteed onions and tomato sauce. Sundays rated roast chicken or fricasseed rabbit, both of which we raised ourselves, along with the mashed potatoes. There were some vegetables: mostly whatever was available from our own extensive garden.

What there wasn't money for was furniture, carpets and rugs, or many clothes. As I mentioned before, I lived in a shabbiness I was too embarrassed to share with school mates. Since I didn't feel I could invite anyone to my home, I simply didn't make friends.

Except for Emily. I don't remember how it happened that we became teenage friends. Most likely it was because we began to walk home from school together. I received a nickel in the morning for the city bus. The end of the bus line was conveniently right in front of my neighbor's house. It took me to about a mile from school. I carried my lunch in a brown paper bag, never a lunch box. The walk home was about three miles, maybe more, rain or shine. Emily lived in South Pasadena, so she could walk right by my house and continue on to hers another mile and a half or so.

I can't imagine in today's world that parents expect their children to walk several miles home from school, but for me there was no other alternative. There was no extra money. For some reason I can't explain, I allowed Emily to come into my home for a glass of water and quick rest, despite my embarrassment about the condition of the house. I knew that Emily came from a better home than I as I had visited a couple of times and met her mother. Emily was well mannered, too. No matter what she might of thought about my living conditions, she never said a word about it to me. It was if she just never saw it.

Emily and I waited for each other to walk home together. Mostly she talked and I listened. Once I got hold of some cigarettes and started puffing on one as we headed home. She told me I looked like a chimney stack. I threw the cigarette away and never smoked again. Emily was my only friend and I didn't want to displease her.

When I graduated from high school I went off to the Air Force and spent four years on active duty. When I returned home I contacted Emily. She invited me to her wedding, and I went. Afterwards I told her I had come out as a lesbian. After all, she was my only friend in high school, and I wanted to be honest with her. I never heard from her again.

PART 2

SIGNIFICANT EVENTS OF MY YOUNGER LIFE

8

Precocious? You Think?

I wasn't a child who played with dolls. Tractors, balls and rode tricycles maybe, but not dolls. I eschewed dresses as much as the rules would allow. Remember, back in my school days little girls had to wear dresses. I fought my mother over dresses from a very early age, preferring jumpers, shorts, pants–what ever wasn't a dress. I guess you could legitimately say I was a "tom-boy."

But I did have one doll that I loved. Literally. She was a soft baby doll. Even her head was soft, no hard spots at all. We were inseparable. Her name was Rosie, and she was my lover from the time I was about five years old. Yes, I mean what you're thinking.

In the privacy of my bed I would turn over on my stomach, tuck little Rosie between my legs and masturbate with her. I'm not trying to fake you out about the age I started masturbating, and I don't remember exactly how it all got started. But I have clear memories of this wonderful pleasure from a time that most psychologists would say is pre-sexual cognizance.

My mother once caught me masturbating with Rosie, and she was taken away from me. I quickly figured out how to bundle up the sheet and blanket enough to gain the traction I needed on my clitoris to reach climax. I was addicted!

I even used a younger neighbor boy behind the house in the middle of the day. He was fully clothed and I was only six, but I suppose that would still make me a "sexual predator." Considering my age at the time, I would prefer to think of it as sexual experimentation. However in my subconscious I must have realized that was an unacceptable action, and I never used another child again.

Somewhere along the line I got Rosie back. I must have promised my mother I wouldn't do it again, but of course I did, a bit more discretely.

As I got older, I discovered the soft bodies of women, and that was much nicer. Now that I have no partner and no longer seek satisfaction in one-night stands, I have a vibrator as a companion. Don't kid yourselves that older women are no longer sexual simply because of their age. There may be something to the old adage "use it or lose it." I can only say I haven't stopped reaching climaxes yet.

9

The Lesson of Mrs Padfield

Soon after my brother died we moved, once more, to a different house in Pasadena, the city of my birth. My aunt Ruby and uncle Glen, my father's younger brother, lived in this house. The day they moved out, we moved in. All-in-all the Beers' rented this house long enough to have purchased it, but never did. I lived there until I left for the Air Force at age eighteen.

When we moved in, we also inherited a live-in, Mrs. Padfield. She was an older blind lady who had rented a room from my uncle, and then from us. She stayed in the front bedroom which was directly across the livingroom from the dining room table. She could get herself to the table for meals without assistance, if not always in a straight line. My mother would cut up her food in bite-size pieces so she could eat it with a spoon.

Mrs. Padfield was very quiet. She read books in braille and listened to the radio. She was only a few steps away from the bathroom and could handle herself there as well. Except for washing her clothes, providing meals, and cleaning her room once in a while, we didn't do much else for her. Occasionally someone from the Braille Institute would come and visit, usually bringing her more books and taking away the ones she had finished. She also had a younger friend or relative that visited once in a while, but remember, I was pretty young at the time and didn't pay too much attention.

Still, I've always wondered if Mrs. Padfield influenced me in ways I never realized. The rent paid for her wasn't very much and probably didn't cover more than her food and utilities. I can't imagine it added anything to my father's pocket, even though we were pretty poor ourselves.

I believe keeping Mrs. Padfield fed and taken care of in her older, blind years was a charitable act on the part of my parents, and believe me, I don't think of my parents in any charitable way. I also think that one act, if none others, rubbed off on me in a way that has affected my life.

I don't mean to be egotistical, but I've lived my life as positively as I could. I've given of myself, mostly in the lesbian community. I've been known for being extremely honest, and that has applied with myself as well. I've never accumulated much money. When I could I've given it to causes I believed in, which are hardly ever main-stream charities, but those less well supported: animals, lesbians, the community.

Somehow I absorbed the concept that helping others was a good thing. I have no idea if it subconsciously tracks back to Mrs. Padfield, but I learned it somewhere!

10

My Childhood Contribution to World War II

I was eight years old on Pearl Harbor Day, December 7, 1941. My remaining brother joined the army, one sister became Virginia the riveter, my other sister served up meals to soldiers, my mother knitted olive green sweaters for the Red Cross to hand out to soldiers, and my father, having been too young for WWI and two old for WWII, became a volunteer fireman for the City of Pasadena. Pat and I collected newspapers.

I lived around the corner from Pat, who was a couple of years older than me. We'd pull an old wagon around the neighborhood knocking on doors and asking for newspapers. Then we'd bring them back to my place, tie them up with string in bundles and store them in our rickety old garage.

During the summer when there was no school, we'd do this nearly every day, working farther and farther away from our home base. Before long, we were working as much as a mile from home! You understand, we didn't get many newspapers from any one house. Not everybody was home or opened the door. My memory is that we felt pretty good about getting a wagon load, or one bundle, on any given day. And not all of our time was spent on collecting old newspapers. We were kids; we did other kid things.

But we kept getting newspapers, bundling them up, and stashing the bundles in the garage. Then one day, lo and behold, there was no more room in the corner of the garage my dad had assigned to us. We were very proud of ourselves.

Being a gardener, my dad owned a truck. One Saturday he and Pat and I loaded up the truck with all the bundles of newspapers and my dad took them off to the collection center. The papers filled the truck to overload which had to be tied down they were piled so high. It seemed to us kids like a billion pounds. It turned out to be something more realistic like a few hundred pounds. But that was all right; Pat and I had done our part for the "war effort." We had persevered day after day pulling that old wagon blocks and blocks and blocks and had filled up a whole truck with old newspapers.

Then we went back to being kids again.

I could never have guessed then that when a few years had passed and I had become an adult, I would be stationed in Germany as occupation troops for this same war.

11

The Broken Window Incident

One day when I was about ten, my two older sisters began to tease me and eventually locked me out of the house. There were three entrances: the front door, a door off my sleeping room, and the backdoor which led to the kitchen and was inside the back porch which housed the washer and ice box. Yes, at that time we still had an ice box, not a refrigerator. I had tried all the doors and was getting more and more angry that I couldn't enter my own house. My sisters kept teasing me from inside the kitchen. The kitchen door had a glass window so I could see my sisters, but not get to them. They should have known better because they were nine and eleven years older than me.

My temper got away from me and I began to hammer my fists on the wooden door just below the window. My right hand struck too high, hitting the glass and shattering it into the kitchen. In the process, I cut my right forearm. The scar I still have is slightly less than 3/4 of an inch long, but that's a big cut to a kid. In my childhood there was no such thing as running off to a doctor for stitches, so my mother cleaned it out, poured Tincture of Mercurochrome in it (which stung like hell) and bandaged it up.

When my father came home and saw the broken window, he turned me over his knee and spanked me with his hand. It was the only time my father ever struck me. Was he concerned I was cut? No, he was just upset I had broken a window which he would need to spend money to repair. As far as I know, my sisters were never chastised for locking me out of the house and teasing me until I was in a rage.

It was my mother that usually did the punishment. I can't honestly say I was spanked that many times as a child, but there were a couple of times I didn't think I deserved it, and that bothered me. My mother was five feet, two inches tall. By the time I was my early teens I matched her height. One day I was later getting home than she thought I should be, and she didn't know where I was. When I did arrive back to the house she was upset, whether from fear or anger or a combination of both, I don't know. But for the first time ever, she took a wooden hanger to the back of my legs. Now that really hurt! When she was finished I stood up, looked at her, and said to my mother, "That is the last time you will ever spank me."

She must have believed me. She never suggested corporeal punishment again.

12

A Rose Is a Rose

I understand my father owned a nursery in the early 1930's, but lost it during the Great Depression. That was about the time I was born. The story I heard from my childhood was that when he was twelve years old it was necessary for him to go to work full time to help support his family. He had very little education, through the sixth grade only, and began working in agriculture. One job or another, it was all he ever knew.

So when he lost the nursery and became unemployed, he began hiring out to individuals as a gardener, mostly in the City of San Marino where, even during a depression, there were people who had enough money to hire a gardener. Eventually he built up a very good clientele, but that's not what this memory is about.

When I reached ten or so I started going to work with my dad during summer school breaks. They were long days as dad worked longer hours in the summertime when he had more daylight. But frankly I didn't work all that hard. I could rake leaves, trim dead flowers, bring him light tools from his truck, and pull weeds. I don't remember him ever pushing me to work harder, and appeared to like the company.

However he had one yard he took care of whose owner would pay me a dollar to spend a couple of hours digging dandelions out of her front lawn each week. For some reason, the woman liked me, short haircut, dirty jeans, baby butch stance and all.

Along with mowing lawns, planting, fertilizing and general clean up gardeners do, my father would experiment with cross-pollination of various flowers. He frequently won prizes for his camellias in flower shows, under the property owner's name, of course. He even had one residence in San Marino that was regularly on the Garden Walking Tour. At the home where he created award-winning camellias, he also grew cymbidiums in the ground,

which the Orchid Society said was impossible. Well, they looked like the
were growing in the ground. The trick is you plant the entire pot in the
ground. Cymbidiums need to be root bound to flower. If they were planted
in the ground without the pot, the roots would continue to grow, but they
would never flower. This is your gardening lesson for the day. Anyway, not
bad for a guy who never got beyond the sixth grade.

At the house where I was the dandelion-killer, he created a hybrid red
rose which the owner named "Miss Jean." No doubt it has died of old age or
been uprooted for new landscaping long ago. But it was very ego-boosting
at the time, and one of the very few things in my childhood I can remember
with a smile. Even though it may be gone now, how many lesbians do you
know who had a rose named after her?

13

My Friendly Tree, the Deodar

In the front yard of the house on South Marengo in Pasadena that I lived in during my teenage years there was a huge deodar, a type of deciduous evergreen related to the pine family. When I say huge, I mean really, really tall. Maybe it seemed taller because I wasn't all that big myself, and very skinny when I was young, but certainly it was twice as high as the roof line of the house.

There is no doubt in my mind today that this tree saved my sanity, and maybe my life.

Fortunately the lower limbs were close enough to the ground I could climb up the tree fairly easily, and did so frequently. One day I asked my dad if I could have some lumber and he allowed me a few old pieces from the back yard. I found a couple of limbs about ten feet off the ground that were reasonably the same level, pulled those boards up, and nailed them to the tree branches. This wasn't a tree house: no sides, no roof, no protection, no hiding place. Just a platform, and I'd climb up and sit. During the day there was enough light to read by. It wasn't all that high, but it was off the ground and above eye level. Many a time I was up there and my mother didn't know where I was. I went there to get away by myself.

When I was feeling really low, I climbed higher up in the tree. I climbed so high the top of the tree would start to bend, and I'd know that was as far as I could go without breaking it. I'd just sit there perched in the fork of branches, alone, quiet, listening to the breeze blowing. Just sit, frequently after dark in the summer when it was warm enough.

My mother knew I went up high in the tree. She knew I was a tom-boy and probably thought I could take care of myself up there without falling out. What she never understood was *why* I went up. To get away from...? Her? The world? Life? I couldn't tell you then; I couldn't tell you now. All I know is it was my place of refuge when I was sad or unhappy or needed to get away. Alone, at the top of the tree, with my arms wrapped around the slim trunk, I sat alone.

The tree is gone now. It was cut down when the city decided to widen the street. Fortunately for me, that was after I had left Pasadena for the military. It will never be a refuge for some other young child or teenager to hide in. But to this day I don't know if I would have survived my teenage years if I hadn't had my deodar to escape to.

I don't have a place to escape to any longer, but I do live alone in a small studio apartment where I can shut myself away from the rest of the world. I have a lesbian library of mysteries, romances and adventures of about a thousand trade paperbacks. I've been known not to leave my apartment all weekend while I reread as many as four books, or maybe watch a ball game on television, or reruns of *Law and Order*, or play cards on the computer. I suspect when I finally retire from work I may lose myself in my books for days on end. Fortunately there's always laundry to do and groceries to buy to get me out of the house once in a while.

14

Why I Hate Cow's Milk!

When I was young I was very, very skinny and my mother thought drinking milk was good for me. Even that nasty goat's milk I was forced to drink in El Monte.

Unfortunately, so did the Pasadena School District.

When I returned to the Pasadena schools, and moved to the South Marengo address which harbored my beloved Deodar, the school I attended (McKinley Elementary) decided I came from a poor family that couldn't afford to feed me correctly and that was why I was so thin.

They were right about being from a poor family, but I always had enough to eat, unlike my older brothers and sisters during the depression. My sister Anne told me that she and Virginia were sometimes so hungry when they were sent to bed that they would sneak out the window and pull carrots from the garden to eat raw. She said if mom had ever known, they would have been severly punished as, she believed, our mother had every carrot accounted for future meals.

I was thin because...I was thin. At least by my time my father had good jobs and could adequately provide food on the table, even though we always suplemented it with fruit and vegetables from the garden, and chickens and rabbits we raised. I suspect I wore off much of the calories I consumed in worry and internal nervousness. I was not a happy child or teenager.

For my "well being" the school decided I would be called out of class twice a day to go to the cafeteria and consume a pint of milk. Can you imagine how that made me feel? The school was pointing out to everyone in the class I was poor and undernourished and needed welfare. I would say any food value in the milk was dissipated instantly by the energy used to hate the people who were doing this to me.

This milk supplement started in elementary and carried over to junior high school. And I did it; I followed the authority of the school, no matter how embarrassed I was or how it made me feel. My mother never interceded for me and I was never sure if she even knew it was happening. I certainly never spoke to her about it. I never spoke to her about anything.

Then, when I entered the ninth grade and my name was called out in the morning to go to the cafeteria for milk, I said, "No." I never went again, and soon everyone but me forgot it ever happened.

To this day I can't abide the taste of regular cow or goat milk. Offer me buttermilk, cottage cheese, cheese, cream cheese, yogurt, chocolate milk. But please, don't put a glass of regular milk in front of me.

15

The Girls Athletic Association

I was (of course!) very athletic in high school. I won letters in softball (catcher), basketball (guard), field hockey (goalie), and badminton. I didn't play tennis and I didn't then or now know how to swim. The problem was, I won letters over several seasons, but I had no sweater to put them on. That's The Sweater, which meant you belonged to The Sweater Club.

You could say I wasn't very popular. You might have gotten that hint from my having only one friend in high school. By necessity I was a loner, and that had carried over from elementary school. I did well as far as grades in class were concerned without hardly trying, but I definitely flunked relationships.

Proof of my athletic ability was counted in the number of letters I won. But when it came to being elected to The Sweater Club, that was something else again. That was a measure of popularity. For three years I attended the yearly fancy dinner for The Sweater Club when they "tapped" the girls who were elected for that year. For three years I sat around the dinner table for that ceremony hoping this would be the year they'd accept me. They never did.

I never let on it mattered me, not to anyone, not at school or at home, or to the day I'm writing this. But it did.

I joined the Air Force right out of high school which required a couple of letters of recommendation. One was from the head of the girls athletic department who was also responsible for approving those accepted to The Sweater Club. The letter she provided me for the recruiter was not glowing, but it didn't stop my entry into the military.

I returned from active duty four years later, and spent a few years working before I took my G.I. Bill and started my education toward a college degree. I went back to Pasadena City College where I had graduated from high school.

Only once did I drop into the athletic department. My nemeses had retired and the head of the department was now a teacher who had actually befriended me when I was there in high school. She asked if I was going to come back and play sports.

I was in a relationship then, but that wasn't the real reason I declined her invitation. I knew I was significantly older, and had learned to be a bit more sociable in the years since I'd left there, but no way could I face The Sweater Club dinner. Being passed over for The Sweater hurt when I was a teenager, but facing the possibility it might happen again as an adult would have been absolutely humiliating. As much as I loved sports, I was not willing to take that chance

16

What Is A Poet?

I mentioned my sister Virginia and I wrote poems for her Sunday School class. By then I'd been writing "poetry" for a while. I don't have any copies or memories of the contents of the poems I wrote with my sister, but I do have the first complete poem I put on paper myself, at age seven.

That first poem is pretty simple, more like a nursery rhyme. Over the next ten years I wrote several poems, which are included in an addendum to this autobiography. The ones I wrote as a teenager are pretty morose and reflect my personal depression and anger. But they were a way I could unburden myself from the dire thoughts I had of life, what was going on around me, my parents, and all that jazz that teenagers abhor. My seventeenth year was my most prolific, supplying nearly half of all the poetry I ever wrote.

I can't imagine anyone in the lesbian community who knows me would think of me as a poet, but I have enjoyed that side of me that very few women know about. The few poems I've written as an adult have been love stuff, but are definitely the best of my work. I don't claim any of it is very good, but if you're interested, check it out. Maybe you can actually see my progression through life in my poetry and songs!

PART 3

THE AIR FORCE YEARS

17

We're Off To See the World! (Or Not)

The day I was eighteen my father did something he never, ever did. He took off from work. Why? To sign my papers to join the Air Force.

Back then, in 1951, which was only three years after Congress signed the act into law which allowed women to join the regular services (rather than an auxilliary branch), a women under twenty-one had to have parental approval to join the military. Women, of course, were not able to make these kinds of decisions on their own before the day they were twenty-one. Men could join up at eighteen, or younger with their parent's consent. Women were different.

I had graduated from high school in June but didn't become eighteen until October. During the summer I had gone to the recruiting office, taken preliminary tests and generally bugged the hell out of the local recruiter. I was ready to go! However all of my suggestions made no difference. The sergeant was very patient, and wanted to recruit me, but there was nothing he could do before I was eighteen.

On my actual birthday my father drove me to the main recruiting office in Los Angeles and I took the official entry examination. To join the Air Force you had to score a minimum of eighty percent on their test; they would take you into the Army at seventy percent. I scored fairly high in the ninety percent range and was told I was one of the highest scores every recorded in Los Angeles at that time.

They gave me a physical. There was a small problem. At five foot, five and a half inches, the chart said I had to weigh a minimum of one hundred ten pounds. I weighed about one hundred eight pounds. I passed the rest of the physical with flying colors. I was told to be sure I "made the weight" by the day I raise my hand, and I'd be accepted. My dad signed the papers.

At that point the recruiter asked me when I would like to actually enlist and leave for basic training. My response was, "I'm ready, how about tomorrow." After he blinked a couple of times he said, "How about a week from Monday. That'll give you time to settle things." I knew I had nothing to settle, but it's hard to argue with a large man in uniform when you're barely eighteen. As it turned out I was eighteen and ten days old when I officially joined the Air Force.

The recruiter gave me a list of clothing and items I was to pack for the trip. It wasn't a very long list. You know, toothbrush, underclothes, etc. After all, when I got to basic training the Air Force would provide me with nearly everything I'd be wearing for the next four years.

The appointed Monday I arrived at the recruiting station with a small suitcase and one hell of a lot of butterflies. I was naive, to say the least. At eighteen I had never had a job, not even a summer one. I'd never been on a train before and knew I was going to spend the next two days on the tracks to San Antonio, Texas. I had never been out of the State of California. In fact, except for the lunch counter at Woolworth's, I had eaten only one meal in a restaurant!

There was also the question of weight. I had done my best to gain two pounds in the previous ten days. I ate bananas for breakfast that day, and I drank a lot of water just before getting on the scale. It registered one hundred nine and a half pounds. The airman weighing me looked at the scale, looked at me and wrote on my record: one hundred, ten pounds! Young, eager and a high test score, they really wanted me.

Fortunately for me there was one other women who was going to basic training from Los Angeles the same day I was. She was in her mid-twenties and, compared to me, very sophisticated. She took me under her wing for the trip and two days later I arrived unharmed at Lackland Air Force Base in San Antonio, Texas, scared and eager all at the same time

18

The Ups and Downs of Basic Training

True to their word, when I arrived at Lackland Air Force Base the Air Force took over my life. Women arrived from all over the United States (including one from Alaska who turned out to be a friend) to make up the four squadrons that started basic training at the same time. I was assigned to the 43rd Squadron with training to last six weeks. The object was to turn me into an "airman" who would follow orders, behave as a military person, and absorb at least rudimentary basics of why I had enlisted.

I had decided at twelve to join the military when I became old enough to do so, and then to become a police woman after that. This was step one, but right off the bat I began to have troubles meeting the goals the Air Force had for me.

Everyone says the first duty they receive is latrine duty, right? Can't be true as only two people are assigned to that duty, but it really was *my* first duty. I had a week of cleaning the latrine (bathroom) every day until the fixtures shined. They inspect it daily and you'd better pass or you'd have to start all over and get a mark, called a demerit, ticked off against your name. Enough marks meant extra duty.

Everything in basic training has to shine: the fixtures in the latrine, your boots, the buttons on your uniform, the floor, your teeth. If it can shine, it had better shine brightly. And, everything must be ultra clean and neat: you, your clothes, your room, your footlocker. You don't pass inspection? Another tick towards extra duty.

You hear rumors about cleaning the floor with a toothbrush? True!

You hear rumors about marching in formation everywhere? True!

You hear rumors about your bed having to be made so tight (with square corners) the Lieutenant can bounce a quarter on it? True!

You hear rumors about marching to breakfast, lunch, dinner and every place in between, spending more time getting to the dining hall (mess) and waiting in line than they give you time to eat? True!

You hear rumors of "if you take it, you eat it" at mess. True! When you turn in your metal tray for washing it gets inspected. It had better be empty. Remember I had a problem meeting my weight limit when I enlisted? By the end of six weeks I'd gained eight pounds. No worry about the minimum weight anymore!

A typical day in basic training, also known as boot camp, is split up between classroom work, learning to march, assigned duties, and keeping you, your uniforms and your room in tip top shape. You have very little personal time. Lights out is early at night, and reveille is early in the morning. Once in a while you even have to be up earlier to *stand* reveille. That means standing at attention at daybreak while the American Flag is being raised over the base. Or if you're really lucky you get to stand taps, which is when the flag is being taken down. No matter if it's raining, or snowing, or still ninety degrees at dawn as I have experienced in San Antonio during the summer, you stand without moving. The woman next to you faints? You stand without moving while she falls to the ground. It's called discipline.

You get marched to chapel on Sunday for a non-denominational Christian service unless you're Jewish, which has it's own service. There were no other choices, like atheist, Buddhist, Muslim, or simply not attending.

My problem was that I really didn't like to be bossed around and told what I could do and not do twenty-four hours a day. I should have thought about this in advance, but I didn't. Consequently I kept getting into trouble.

It didn't help any that I was going through the throes of coming out, which you absolutely could not do then without instant dishonorable discharge. I had fallen in love with my instructor the day I entered boot camp and she yelled "Line up." Her name was Ramona, she was cute and she looked great in her crisp uniform. Needless to say nothing ever came of that!

After all, I didn't actually know what falling in love meant. I didn't have my first sexual encounter with a woman until more than a year later and several thousand miles from San Antonio. I only knew I took every opportunity that came my way to impress Ramona. I even took to sleeping on a mattress outside her barracks room on the pretense I was...what? Protecting her? Being near her? She put up with it for a couple of weeks and then sent me back to my own bed. What a disappointment; I hadn't had to make that bed for two weeks!

Then there was the day I was leading a handful of other trainees from my squad in practicing drills. We were marching between the barracks and really trying to be quiet. But not quiet enough as it turned out. An officer came out, shut us down and reported me to my commander. Another tick against my record.

You enter basic training with no stripes on your sleeve and, for most trainees, when you complete bootcamp successfully, you graduate and receive your first stripe. I graduated, but I didn't get that first chevron.

During training I took a battery of aptitude tests so the Air Force could place me in a job after boot camp that, hopefully, I'd be happy with and could do well. At the time I was in basic training only about fifty percent of the jobs listed for the Air Force were available to women. Nothing to do with combat or front lines was considered appropriate. No airplane engine mechanics, no firefighters, no firearms instructors. What was considered appropriate for women were mostly clerical jobs, whether that was in an office or hospital or payroll accounting.

My aptitude test scores were outstanding in all categories! When I went to my interview late in basic training, I was told I qualified for any job available, and was asked what job I would like to do. I didn't know how to do anything job-wise and hadn't even thought about what I might like to train for because, from my point of view, all the really good jobs were restricted to men. I was asked, "How would you like to go to Radio Mechanics School?" That didn't sound too bad to me. I knew nothing about radio mechanics, but I figured it wouldn't be in an office and I wouldn't have to wear a class-A uniform (skirt) but could be comfortable in fatigues (pants).

Another problem arose. Remember I mentioned when we first arrived they issued us uniforms? Well they didn't have an overcoat to fit me; it was on back-order and hadn't arrived yet. Radio Mechanics School was in the southern part of the State of Illinois. It was winter and it was snowing there. I was given a choice: take the Radio Mechanics School in Illinois in winter without an overcoat, or stay at Lackland AFB until I received the overcoat and take the first assignment that came up, no matter what or where it was!

This California girl didn't fancy Illinois in winter without the proper attire, so I opted for the second choice, leaving my future in a state of unknown.

One by one after graduation my squadron mates began shipping out to their new assignments. The bodies still living in the barracks, now between training sessions until the new year arrived, dwindled down to myself and two others. I was assigned a temporary job on base in the accounting office where I toted up lists of something I can't remember and worked on reports that probably had no value. Our squad had drawn KP (which stands for Kitchen Police or cleanup in the mess) for Thanksgiving. I was still waiting for my overcoat at Christmas; I drew KP duty. I was still there at New Years; I was put on KP duty. I was beginning to think my main job for the Air Force was going to be cleaning up in the mess hall on every holiday that existed!

But no, early in January my overcoat arrived! I was called into the assignment office. "Congratulations," I was told. "You're going to March Air Force Base in California to do on-the-job-training in supply."

Great! The first time I get out of California it lasts three months and I'm sent back to within a few miles of my home town. How the hell was I going to see the world that way?

19

March Air Force Base: First Assignment (Too Close To Home)

I received a two week leave before I had to report to my new duty station in Riverside, barely more than a stone's throw away from where I was born in Pasadena. I spent it with my parents who then drove me out to the base on Sunday, my dad's one day off from work.

I reported on Monday morning to my assignment in base supply where the sergeant in charge looked at my transfer orders, looked at my arm where there was no Private First Class stripe as he expected there to be right out of basic training, and told me my first duty each morning was to make coffee. I told him I didn't drink coffee and didn't know how to make it, thinking this would get me out of that stereotypical job. Wrong! He informed me he would show me one time, did so, and I made coffee in the morning for as long as I was there.

I wasn't a feminist then, maybe I never became one. But having to make coffee each morning was not my idea of what I had joined the military for! I grumbled a bit and did it. Remember, one of the things I *did* learn in basic training was there were consequences to not obeying orders.

On-the-job training means just that. You know nothing when you get there and as something needed to be done, someone taught you how to do it. It was also expected that the next time it came up, you'd remember. In supply that means such things as handing out clean sheets once a week, bundling up the dirty ones, and counting them when they come back clean. You're always short on the clean count. You give them one hundred sheets, consider yourself lucky if you get back ninety-eight and they're all full size (meaning the laundry didn't tear one in half to make two, neither of which will now fit on a bed).

And there was a lot of record keeping. Supplies came in, supplies went out, everything was covered by a piece of paper which then had to be translated into the inventory books. Remember, this was before computers, everything was done on paper. In the five months I spent at March AFB, I learned the basics of supply, including how to make reasonably decent coffee.

But there was one thing I wasn't allowed to do that was a function of the supply office. I couldn't check guns out or in. I was a woman; women were not allowed to handle firearms. All enlisted men had a rifle; all officers had a side arm, usually a .45 caliber hand gun. Women could not be trusted with guns, or at least that's how the regulation made me feel. Most women didn't care. It also meant they didn't have to clean them. I cared because I felt I was being treated differently than other enlisted personnel because of my gender, and that pissed me off. I suspect this was the beginning of my seeking equal rights for women, even if I didn't realize it at the time. All in all, my time went pretty well. I learned my job in supply and funtioned quite efficiently.

I also made a few friends, especially one woman. She, her boyfriend, another guy and myself formed a foursome that did a few weird and illegal things together. Like we'd steal oranges from a commerical orchard, and siphon gasoline at night out of the trucks in the motor pool to fill the boyfried's car. They were all misdemeanors, but the Air Force wouldn't have liked it if we'd been caught. This was something very new to me who had been a law-abiding child, except for the sling shot the police took away from me when I was about twelve.

I went home on a weekend pass and when I came back on Monday, I found out in my absence my three pals had been driving too fast, lost control of their vehicle and rolled it several times. All three were in the hospital; they were lucky no one was killed. I took that as a sign and decided I was the lucky one to have taken a pass that particular weekend, or I would have been in the car with them. They all survived and eventually went back to their duties, but we were never close friends again.

Not long after that I was called into the Adjutant's office. He asked me if I would like to be reassigned to Offutt Air Force Base out of Omaha, Nebraska. I told him no, I wasn't interested. I was enjoying my assignment in supply, and had actually earned my missing stripe! He said that was too bad, because I was going.

Female airmen live in their own barracks and have personnel assigned to run that complex, including a Commander. Apparently I had caught my Captain's attention before she shipped out to a new assignment. She had become the Commander of the women's unit at Offutt AFB and had asked for me by name, rank and serial number. When an officer requests your reassignment to her station, you go.

I always wondered why the Adjutant bothered to ask me if I wanted to be transferred if the decision had already been made to send me and the orders were in process of being cut. Probably some male power trip.

20

Offutt Air Force Base: The Tribulations of Growing Up Fast

I arrived at Offutt AFB (affectionately also known as Awful AFB) in June via a long train ride from California to Nebraska. I hadn't been away from home but eight months and had taken my third train trip: to and from San Antonio, and then to Omaha.

Offutt is headquarters for the Strategic Air Command, the kick-butt section of the Air Force. Thus it had lots of generals and high ranking men and women roaming the base. It thought of itself as premiere and expected everyone to act top notch. Keep this in mind as you read.

I hadn't wanted to go to Offutt, but I really liked the Captain who had requested my transfer and was looking forward to working with her. I had been sent there to be the supply person for the women's barracks, doing all the supply stuff I had been doing in California, but for women only. That had great appeal to me. However when I got there my Captain was gone! She had been replaced by a First Lieutenant who was much younger, backed up by a Second Lieutenant who didn't take to me from the very moment she met me. I didn't stand a chance from the very beginning.

Arriving in Omaha in early Summer, I experienced the muggy heat I wasn't accustomed to in Southern California. And bugs! I never knew such bugs existed! If you stayed in the barracks you sweltered. If you went outdoors, even after dark, you were bitten and annoyed by flying insects. What, I asked, are those flashes on the horizon? Heat lightning I was told. Huh?

Then, before I finally left Offutt in December six months later, I experienced my first blizzard. I had to shovel my way to the barracks doors and then shovel the snow off the pathway to the mess hall for the cooks to get in to fix breakfast, and finally clear the walkways around the compound so everyone could get to breakfast and off to work. I learned to shovel snow in a hurry!

Meanwhile, between the bugs and the blizzard, I spent six months getting in trouble. And here you thought I'd learned my lesson.

Because I was staff in the women's squadron, I got a room at the end of one barrack. Most women slept in double decker cots in a open room, about fifty to a barrack. I made friends with a women who absolutely hated living in the open conditions, not having space or furniture of her own or room for her makeup. I got permission for her to share my room. No, we weren't lovers (remember, I'm still an innocent here); she had a boyfriend. That lasted for a while without too much difficulty, except she never cleaned up after her makeup and the desk we had in the room was always covered with dusting powder (or something).

Then one day I was asked by two women in my barrack if they could sleep on the floor in my room. I suspect these two *were* lovers, but never asked any questions. One of them was so butch looking I was, and still am, surprised she didn't get booted out. If they ever did anything together, I don't know about it. Eventually the situation came to the attention of the commander and we were interrogated. I swore nothing was happening between anybody, but it didn't matter. Rumors had started and I lost my room.

The barracks were pretty full, so I asked and obtained permission to live by myself in my supply room. I had a locker for my clothes, slept on a pile of mattresses, had a bathroom with a shower at my disposal, and was never late to work! That lasted about three months when the Second Lieutenant started agitating that it wasn't seemly for me to be living in my supply room, the place I also worked all day. I believe she just wanted to hassle me. I certainly was shut off from everyone else with very little interaction. I was sent back to the barracks and had to spend the rest of my time at Offutt in a top bunk.

One day I was in the mess hall eating lunch when someone yelled, "Fire!" I left my meal and ran outside to find the dumpster was indeed on fire. I grabbed a hose and poured water into the trash container. I could hear sirens in the background but didn't wait for the firemen. They were there pretty quickly, but by the time they arrived, I had doused the flame. I left it up to them to determine whether or not the fire was really out. While they were checking the situation over, I went back into the mess hall to finish my lunch. However, while I was out saving the wooden headquarters building next to the dumpster from going up in flames, someone had picked up my lunch and thrown it away! I thought I was a hero, but I went hungry until dinner.

In the military there is an extensive sports program. In season you had teams for baseball, basketball, bowling: the three Bs. I learned to bowl at the lanes on base and once scored, in practice, nine strikes in a row. We would get time off from regular duty to train, and trips to other bases to play. Usually the Air Force would provide us with an airplane which was being used for flight training anyway. Towards the end of my six months at Offutt I had gone off with our basketball team to play against the women in Oklahoma City. I can't remember if the team won or lost, but I lost.

After the game we all went to the PX and had a beer. I didn't drink really, but did have part of one while we waited for an airplane to take us back to our home base. Whenever there is space on an aircraft, any military person, of any service, can fly free. There were several men on the plane besides our team, and among them a male sailor who was seated next to me. I got friendly with the sailor and eventually stretched out with my head in his lap. That's it; nothing more. But someone else made a remark to the Lieutenant who was our chaperone (not my nemesis Adjutant) about how quickly a sailor can get out of the thirteen buttons on his pants, and I was instantly in trouble. When the plane landed back at our home base and everyone disembarked, I said goodbye to the sailor by kissing him, right there on the tarmac. I was already in trouble, so I figured what the hell.

The next day I got called into the commander's office and was informed they were considering court marshaling me. I had gotten my second stripe by then, and they were determined to take it away. My conduct, I was told, was "unbecoming to an airman." To make a long story shorter, I eventually agreed to give up a stripe under Article 15 of the Uniform Code of Military Justice and was busted back from Corporeal to Private First Class. However my Commander and Adjutant never knew the laugh was really on them. This lesbian was disciplined for kissing a *man*?

After I got busted I asked for reassignment. From my point of view, it could be to anywhere other than where I was. From my Commander's point of view, it seemed like a good idea, too. In October I had turned nineteen, a magic age to the Air Force as it qualified me for overseas duty. In December, right after the blizzard, I was told I was being transferred. My new assignment? Germany! I was finally going to see some of that world I was wondering about.

21

The Men In My Life

Yes, there were a few (a very few) men in my world. It appears to me I spent the first year in the Air Force trying to prove to myself I wasn't a lesbian. It worked! Of course in the opposite direction, meaning at the end of that year there was no doubt in my mind about my sexual orientation, although I had not yet made love with a woman.

While stationed at March AFB I frequently dated a guy from West "God Damn" Virginia. His declaration, not mine. Mostly I double dated with a friend. I mention our escapades earlier. The one behavior I did not participate in was having sex, although I knew my friend was doing so. West "God Damn" Virginia and I kissed, our bodies got pretty intimate fully clothed, but that was all.

The six months I was stationed at Offutt I briefly dated three different airmen. And I do mean briefly.

My first "date" I went out one evening for a two hour car ride with a black sergeant. It was just a car ride, nothing more. I mention his skin color only because after that one short ride, I started getting phone calls in the barrack from a whole bunch of black men I had never met! I grew up in a mixed neighborhood and could care less about a person's skin color. But getting anonymous calls from strangers, all of whom were from a specific race and making crude suggestions, set me back on my heels. I never understood what triggered all those calls, but I didn't go riding with the sergeant again.

I went out for pizza one night with a young man whose parents were from India. He pulled out a condom after dinner while we were sitting in his car. I guess he figured a couple of slices of pizza bought him a fuck. Wrong! Didn't happen; didn't see him again.

Then one day I consciously decided I needed to find out what fucking was all about. After all, I certainly knew about masturbation, having indulged myself since five years old. So I went out on a date with George solely to have sex with a man. We went to a deserted somewhere in his pickup truck. As men go he was a pretty nice guy, and not too rough with me. After some preliminary petting and kissing, and with no objection from me, he laid me on the front seat and unzipped his pants. He pulled off my panties and I opened my legs for him in cooperation. He couldn't have asked for more except one thing: I tried to cooperate, but my body didn't! I was still a virgin, and my muscles clamped down so hard against his attempt to penetrate me that he literally couldn't get inside. I swear it was not conscious on my part, but my body (or my subconscious) was not willing to let him in.

I even tried again the next day when he took me out to another deserted location. This time he laid out a blanket on the ground giving us more space than in the truck and, presumably, making it more comfortable. Forget it! Didn't work! Same result as the night before! I'll give George some credit. If he was sexually frustrated he neither blamed me or masturbated himself in front of me. He even attempted to "give me some pleasure" in his words with his fingers, but he was too rough for me and that was not successful either. As I said, he was a nice guy, but I never saw him again.

There were a couple of other men I went out with in Germany, but never allowed myself to get into a sexual situation. Obviously I was meant to be a lesbian, and if I didn't think so (which of course I did), my body was absolutely sure.

There is one more guy I need to write about, Jon. He was not a GI, but a reporter for the Chicago-Sun Times. When I left Offutt heading for Germany, I first got a two week leave to go home for a visit. That's standard procedure when you change assignments. I hopped a military plane from Offutt to San Bernardino, one of the closer bases to Pasadena. Jon was on that plane too, heading to Los Angeles.

We were the only two people who had taken the ride on this cargo plane, so it was natural we got to talking. Actually, we had about six hours to talk! In that time period, with no one else around, we got to know quite a bit about each other. He was thirty-two, I was nineteen. We were both unmarried and he never had been. We were both headed for Germany, me for duty and him as a reporter, although he was going to Berlin in the north and I was headed to a base outside Munich in the south. I kissed him goodbye on the flight line in San Bernardino, but this time no one was there to chastise me, never expecting to see or hear from him again. But I did, six months later in Germany.

I received a call in the barrack one day, and there was Jon on the other end telling me he had a few days and was coming from Berlin down to Munich to see me. He was there the next Saturday and we took the local train into Munich and had a couple of drinks, talked and kicked around. He had come most of the way across Germany just to see me, and I began to get a little nervous about it all.

We caught the last train from Munich back to Erding Air Depot about eleven that night, and Jon started to get too serious for me. He was making plans to see me again, he was holding my hand, he was sitting too close. I was beginning to wonder what was going on. So I did the one thing I knew would stop him: I told him I thought I liked women better than men. By then I had (finally) experienced a women sexually, so there really was no question in my mind. Telling him this could have been disastrous for me if he decided to report that to my Captain, but he wasn't that kind of person. He simply nodded sadly and backed off.

I believe if I'd been interested I could have led Jon up to asking me to marry him. Not so much because he loved me, we didn't really know each other that well, but because he was tired of looking for a good fuck, or washing and ironing his own shirts, or just wanted to get married for the sake of getting married now that he was in his thirties. Hell, I wouldn't have been a good lay for him as we already know!

I think of Jon every time some straight male jerk mouths off that I/we are only lesbian(s) because we "can't get a man." There is no question in my mind I could have married Jon if I'd wanted to. After all, a lot of people get married for entirely the wrong reasons. I've always wondered if he found the right woman for him and lived happily ever after. I hope so.

22

Welcome To Germany: First Chance to See "The World"

My enlistment in the Air Force was for four years. I spent three months at Lackland AFB, about five months at March AFB and six months at Offutt AFB. I spent the rest of my four years at Erding Air Depot, Germany, most with the occupation troops for the Second World War. When I was young and collected newspapers for "the war effort," no way would I have ever guessed I would be stationed in Germany before the conflict was over!

Most people who remember anything about WWII know it ended in 1945. But what they don't know or remember, is the United States did not sign a treaty with Germany until 1955, ten years after the war "ended." In the meantime during that ten year period, I grew up, joined the Air Force and was shipped overseas, arriving in January 1953. And what an arrival it was!

Again I had been given two weeks leave before shipping out to Germany. I caught a free flight back to California from Offutt, spent the time at home, and took (another) train all the way to New Jersey with a change of trains in Chicago. When I left Los Angeles at eighteen I was naive, never been on a train, never been out of California, and by the time I was nineteen and three months old I was on my fourth train trip (five days worth sitting up), crossing the entire United States, been in trouble so many times I'd lost count, and was still naive.

I nearly missed my flight out of New Jersey on a Naval aircraft to Europe because I was being shown around by one of the women with whom I had gone through basic training. While we were traipsing around the base, my flight to Germany was called and everybody left the barrack and headed for the plane except me. When I got back to the barrack I discovered no one there and a kindly Navy person informed me my buddies had left for the flight line some time back. I barely made it before my plane took off. Everyone else had already boarded, engines were running, and it was ready to go. Had it taken off without me, I probably would have lost my one remaining stripe.

The flight itself was not luxurious, but it was uneventful. We stopped in the Azores to refuel, the first time I set foot on any "foreign" soil. We refueled again in Scotland, and ended up in Frankfurt, Germany. There were only a couple of other women on the flight, and when we arrived in Frankfurt am Main we were put up at the women's barrack there overnight. I was the only one going on the next day by train to Munich, then to my assignment at Erding.

A few of the women who were stationed in Frankfurt were kind enough to take us newcomers out for a night on the town, or at least to our first beer hall. Beer halls are big in Germany. There were about eight of us sitting around a large table and the other women had lured a young German man to sit with us and were kidding him and flirting with him. They didn't speak German and he didn't speak much English. I believe they were being innocent enough, just intent on having some fun. But the American GIs sitting at the next table were trying unsuccessfully to get the American women's attention, and one GI in particular was getting angrier at being ignored as he got drunker. Suddenly he smashed his beer mug on the head of the German man sitting at our table, splitting open the young man's scalp. Quickly the young German was whisked off to be taken care of, and other Germans working at the beer hall hustled the GI out of the hall. As occupation troops, Americans were not subject to German laws and courts. I always wondered if that GI got the shit kicked out of him, but since I left Munich the next morning, I never found out.

Welcome to Germany!

23

Erding Air Depot: My Home Away from Home

When I reached the air base, my first assignment was to the supply room of the base hospital. Where you work in supply, general, women's barrack, hospital or anywhere else, didn't make a whole lot of difference. Sure the items you handled might be of a new nature (instruments and medicines as well as sheets and blankets), but how you handled them was the same.

My sergeant was a crusty guy in his mid-forties who drank heavily; he was a career enlisted man. From my point of view he was a perfect example of a man who stays in the military all his life because he probably wouldn't make it successfully as a civilian. In the military, with six stripes on his sleeve and more than twenty years of service, he had more power that he would have had elsewhere. He wasn't very efficient. However, when I arrived in his unit, he took one look at my last name and asked, "Has anyone ever called you Suds?" I told him no, and that became my name to him the rest of the time I was in the medical unit.

Like all of my assignments up to this point in the Air Force, I didn't stay but a few months in the hospital supply. I was then transferred to the women's barracks to be their supply person. How about that! I kept being transferred to women's quarters! But unlike my other postings, I spent the next two and a half years, the rest of my time in Germany and the Air Force, in that assignment.

The women's barrack at Erding was unlike any I've ever heard of in the Air Force because we had a women's bar right there under the same roof! On base there's always an Officers Club, and an Enlisted Officers Club, the latter usually restricted to sergeants, three stripes and up. But at Erding we also had a Airmen's Club for those under the rank of sergeant, plus a Women's Club.

Because we were in a foreign country, and one we had defeated at war, the military believed keeping us on base as much as possible was the best way to go.

As an aside, but related to the last thought, when the men went off base on pass or leave, they had to wear their uniforms. But when women left the base, we had to do so in civilian clothes, in order to blend in better. I never got a good explanation of this rule; it just was so.

Back to the bar. We had a German women who was hired to tend the bar, but the best part about it was the lack of dress code and the privacy. Since the bar was physically located at one end of our barrack, only steps from our rooms, we were allowed to come into the bar dressed anyway we wanted, even pajamas if that fit our fancy, except for Wednesday and Saturday nights when the bar was opened for the women to have male guests. No males were allowed in the barrack at all other times, and on those two nights they could only get in the bar with a woman escort.

If one of the men got drunk, he was instantly thrown out into the night to make his way back to his own bed. If one of the women had a little too much to drink it was easy for her friends or the night guard to assist her off to her own room. The bar closed at 10:00 at night and bed check was an hour later. It really worked well and I've always thought the military should think about having women-only bars at all the bases.

We had grand old times in that women's bar. We decorated for the holidays. One Halloween I made up a witch from a dress form, a glass light fixture covered with a witches rubber mask and sporting a black pointed hat, black cloth draped over the form with a broom stick being held out by one draped arm. It was quite effective and greatly appreciated by all. We had beer mugs made up with each woman's name and year when they arrived. We had a place we could be to let our hair down, have a little fun, and not have to fight off men we weren't interested in. Those women who wanted to meet men always had the option to go to the other clubs on base.

I got my second, corporal, stripe back after my supply job moved to the women's barrack. About a year later our First Sergeant completed her tour and left for the U.S. and I was asked if I wanted to take over her job as First Sergeant. She was a Master Sergeant in rank, six stripes on her sleeve; I had two. I was twenty years old and was being asked to take overall responsibility for one hundred and twenty women ranging in age from nineteen to fifty! Of course I said yes. I was asked by my commanding officer if I wanted a temporary promotion to sergeant, three stripes. My response was if they wouldn't respect me with two stripes, they wouldn't respect me with three. My Captain looked at me in surprise and simply said, "OK."

I spent the next year plus as First Sergeant with only minor difficulties, none of which had to do with my age, until I shipped home for discharge. In looking back, my audacity at thinking I could do that job at such a young age and with very little experience, was astounding. But I believe I did as good a job as anyone else could have. I did get my third stripe eventually and was discharged from the regular Air Force as a sergeant.

24

My First Lover (Finally!)

Despite my precocious sexual behavior, I never actually had real sex with a woman until I was nineteen. Her name was Gerry. As it turned out she wasn't a particularly nice person and gave me a hard time. But she was my first woman lover.

After a little experimentation I discovered that having a climax with someone else is far superior to having one with a cloth doll or blanket edge. Not only is there the touchy-feely thing going on with real skin and kisses and juices I hadn't known existed, but the climax itself is way beyond anything I ever imagined.

However, the relationship with Gerry was short-lived. It fully ended the night she was intoxicated, wouldn't go to bed even though the bar had closed and it was past bed-check, and took a swing at me when I was trying to persuade her to behave. At that time I was still in supply but, being staff, it was a bit awkward to say the least. When she took the swing at me, I simply grabbed hold of her upper arms and pinned her against the wall until she settled down. Gerry then informed me she was going to report me as a lesbian. I suspect she thought that threat was to get me to leave her alone so she could do whatever she thought she wanted. The bar was closed anyway, so she couldn't get anything more to drink, and I finally pursueded her to go off to bed.

But this was 1953; lesbians and gays were quickly hustled out of the military in a blink of an eyelash. So first thing next morning I reported the incident to my commander, including the threat that Gerry was going to call me a lesbian. My thinking was if I had any chance at all of getting through this, I might be able to defuse the situation by bringing it up myself. Apparently it worked! I never knew if Gerry did declare I was a lesbian, but

I never heard anything further after my commander told me not to worry about it.

Gerry refused a direct order from an officer not long after that incident and was court-marshaled for that act. I was one of the people present at her act of defiance and had to be a witness against her. I couldn't help but wonder if that would be the point she would bring up my being a lesbian. But she didn't, and she was shipped home soon after her conviction.

Gerry was not my only lover while I was in Germany, but I felt like I'd dodged a bullet with my first one!

25

Sports In the Military

Playing sports in the military meant time off from duty to practice and travel to other bases to compete. Despite the incident at Offutt when I flew off to play basketball and ended up losing a stripe, I jumped into sports feet first with enthusiasm when I got to Germany.

I had learned to bowl at Offutt, but at Erding I got involved with my first bowling league. I was on an all-women team of five bowlers, four of whom were wives of enlisted men! Did they ever notice I dressed differently than they did, even though we had identical bowling shirts? Who knows. Did they ever notice I didn't join their conversations about their husbands or men? Who knows. Did they accept me as a bowler? You bet! I was a better bowler than most of them.

Because enlisted women who bowled were spread out all over Germany with never enough at any one base to put together a league, the system was a bit different than I've since experienced in civilian life. Any enlisted woman who was bowling in any league, would submit her scores each week to a central committee stationed in Wiesbaden, headquarters for our Command. The committee would maintain the averages for all of the women, and at the end of the bowling season, would pick the women with the highest averages to compete in a tournament somewhere in Germany. I went twice to Frankfurt.

Remember, the Air Force thought this was a good thing for our morale and gave us time off from duty to participate. A bowling tournament was worth about a week off from work.

You never knew who you would meet, and never see again. Quickie liaisons were certainly possible, and probable. The biggest problem was finding someplace to have the liaison. Talk about raging hormones making you do stupid things. Invariably we slept in open barracks with no privacy.

We never had any transportation to go off the base, and wouldn't know the area anyway. So you stole a few minutes whenever and wherever you could. Remember, most enlisted women are *not* lesbians. You couldn't count on them assisting you. In fact you'd better be sure they didn't see anything suspicious or they were more likely than not to report you.

I remember at one tournament meeting a women and instantly connecting with her as a lesbian. She was a totally inexperienced one at that, not that I was all that experienced myself. In the little time we had to talk, I found out she had been sexually abused by her father and wasn't interested in men. We found a few minutes in an empty barrack one afternoon when there wasn't anyone around and had a quick sexual encounter. Talk about stupid! Someone could have walked in at any time and both of us would have been out of the Air Force with a dishonorable discharge in record time. But no one did come in and she discovered that she liked what she felt with a woman.

And then there was basketball and baseball. I really wanted to play softball, my very favorite sport. But in my last season in Germany there weren't enough women at Erding AFB who were interested in softball to make up a team to compete. One of the nice rules the military had in Germany was if you wanted to play a sport, and your base didn't have that sport, you were permitted to go and play with the closest base that had, in this case, a softball team. That wasn't all too far for me: it was only to Munich. Except, it was an women's Army team I got to play with. Remember, I got time off to travel to Munich for practice as well as competition.

While I was in Germany, the Air Force had sent me to the base driving school where I learned to drive, got a military license, and purchased a used vehicle. So getting back and forth to Munich was no problem. I made friends with some of the WACs (Women's Army Corps) on the team after they got used to having a WAF (Woman of the Air Force) playing with them. I became intimate with one of them, Susan, and hung out with her and one of her friends, Janice.

After softball season ended, the team, which included me, was given a weekend pass and we all went off to see one of Ludwig's castles which was located in the middle of a lake. Being somewhat adventurous and young, Janice, Susan and I rented a rowboat to take us out to the castle. Of the three of us, only Janice knew how to row or how to swim. Soon after we started off, clouds began to form very quickly. When we were about halfway out to the island, it started to rain and the wind came up rather suddenly. Getting wet was not a problem, but Susan began to panic. She started screaming, stood up in the rowboat, and it began to rock. Janice, who was rowing as hard as she could yelled at Susan to sit down. I was frozen in place convinced, since

I didn't know how to swim, that I was about to die. Frankly, I was damned scared.

Susan did finally sit down and Janice got us to the island just before the last boat for the day back to the mainland was about to leave. We abandoned the rowboat and took the ship back to shore. There we went to the rental office and told them their rowboat was still on the island filling rapidly with water. They smiled and told us not to worry, when the storm was over they'd go pick it up and tow it back. It was not the first time I had experienced a German civilian smile indulgently at an American GI. I was convinced he was thinking: *Too bad they didn't drown.*

Writing about this incident doesn't seem as traumatic as living it. But I tell you, being out in the middle of a lake in a storm, not being able to swim, and having one person in the rowboat in a panic, was the most frightening moment of my life (so far). Neither before nor since have I been that scared. For some reason, Susan and I weren't as friendly after that incident. But what the hell, softball season was over anyway!

26

Gloria

My first "long term" relationship was with Gloria.

One night I had retired in time for bed check, having left Gloria on night duty. Being staff, I had a small single room instead of having to share with one or two other women. Soon after I was in bed, but not yet asleep, Gloria open the door of my room, I thought to do bed check, but walked in and closed the door behind her. She walked over to my bed, leaned down, kissed me, and turned and left the room quickly. Before I could say "Wait," she was already out the door. I looked for an opportunity to speak with her the next day, but never found a time when we were alone. It took several days before I could get her to my room and in private. We became lovers and remained so until she shipped home for discharge.

Gloria was three years older than I and had enlisted a year or so before I did. She was from the East Coast (Massachusetts) and had worked for Western Union before she joined up. Her job with the company was waiting for her when she returned. She had natural blond hair cut at a medium length, and I remember her as about my same height. However she was a very "stiff" person, always tense. At the time she outranked me by a stripe.

You could say Gloria and I had an up and down relationship. Since I had a private room, we were able to spend time together there in relative safety after bed check. We would take leave together and traveled to several countries: Italy, Austria, Liechtenstein, Switzerland, The Netherlands. We took two trips to Italy and two to Holland together. I was much less sophisticated than she, so I let her make all the arrangements and take the lead in traveling. We also made short trips into Munich and other locations in Germany together.

At that time in European hotels, when reservations were made for two women you ended up with two beds in your room, even if you only used one. I remember once, however, when we got to our hotel room rather late,

71

the desk clerk was very embarrassed because he didn't realize from our names we were both women, and he had nothing left to offer but a double bed. We suppressed our smiles and soberly told him that would be all right. What luxury, sleeping in a double bed instead of both of us in a single!

There was one disturbing pattern about our going off together. Just before every planned trip, Gloria and I would have an argument. At this point I have no memory what the arguments would be about. Maybe it was just the tension of traveling and wondering if anyone was noticing how many trips we made together. We'd make up just before departing, and the vacation would turn out just fine.

Gloria and I were coming back from a trip to Italy once when an Italian gentleman joined us in the compartment we had taken. European train accommodations were compartments for six or eight with doors to the outside as well as the inside aisle. Depending on what class you traveled, the compartments were more or less comfortable. The man did not speak English or German, and neither Gloria nor I could speak Italian. But both Gloria and the Italian could speak enough French to carry on some conversation. Although I was just a bystander, comprehending no language but English, I reflected upon how wonderful that people can figure out a way to communicate when they really want to.

There was one thing that bothered me about Gloria's and my sexual relationship. She absolutely refused to make a first move. If I didn't initiate sex, there wouldn't be any. Since I was only twenty, fairly new to lesbian life, and had raging hormones, I always eventually gave in. We even discussed it, and she knew it pissed me off that she didn't want me enough to start the action. It just wasn't part of her personality.

The fire alarm went off in the barrack once in the middle of the night, and it wasn't a drill. Just like our practiced fire drills, everyone rushed out to the clear area behind the barrack and took formation. I grabbed the duty roster and started taking the head count. It was my job to account for every person. When I hit the W's towards the end of the roster and I came to Gloria's name, she didn't answer. I came just short of panicking, shoved the clipboard into the hands of one of my older sergeants and told her to finish the head count. I then rushed into the barrack to find Gloria, not knowing if we had a real fire or not.

She wasn't in her room, and there was actually quite a bit of smoke in the building. I rushed down the hall and out of the other end of the barrack where I found firemen, who had pulled a burning mattress out of a room and were dousing it with water. There was no fire inside the barrack, only smoke.

And there was Gloria, casually standing around in her bathrobe watching the firemen work!

I was furious at her. I reminded her she was supposed to be in formation at the other end of the building and ordered her there. When we got back to the other troops, the sergeant I had pushed the roster onto handed it back to me and gently said, "It's good thing she wasn't at the beginning of the alphabet." Her eyes told me she knew exactly why I had taken off so quickly. To my chagrin she was right. My duty was to look after all the troops, not go running off to find my missing lover.

A small postscript to this fire story having nothing to do with Gloria: there was a heroine connected to the fire. We were pretty relaxed in Germany, and one of the women had a very small, mixed breed dog she kept in her room. The dog was never a problem and no one ever complained. But I'll bet you've guess already: it was the dog that smelled the smoke first, woke up her master who called the base fire department and set off our alarm. The dog was female, of course.

After being lovers for more than a year, Gloria shipped home. I still had some time to go in Germany, but harbored questions as to whether or not we would get together when I was discharged. I received only one letter from her. She had written it aboard the ship taking her home, a few days out from Germany. In it she said the memory of me was fading quickly. That certainly answered my question.

27

Travel and Art In Europe

One of the wonderful aspects of my relationship with Gloria was that we did go on leave (vacation) together and traveled to several different central European countries, as well to some countries more than once. Thus I gained an education I would never have received in any school.

The diversity in cultures in Europe is significantly more widespread than you would first consider in a relative small area of the world, until you experience them. From the friendliness of Hollanders to the neutral surface attitude of the Germans to the expressed dislike of Americans in France, particularly Paris, you cannot disregard the populations attitude toward you while traveling among them.

We freed The Netherlands from German tyrants, and they loved Americans for that. We conquered the Germans and destroyed ninety percent of their cities and industries and in speaking to and interacting with individual Germans, you really wouldn't know how they felt. After all, in occupying their country for ten years, *we* were the tyrants. We freed France, too, and they hated us for doing so and haven't become that friendly in all the years since "The War."

Still, you traveled as much as you could. First you wanted to get away from the military as much as you would any job. Then too, most GIs understood they had this opportunity to see Europe and they wanted to take advantage of it.

And then there's the art!

Paintings, sculpture, friezes, stained glass, architecture competed for attention with mountains, lakes and King Ludwig's castles. Much of the art in Europe was commissioned by Popes and is found in Catholic churches. I'm not a religious person, but I never hesitated to cover my head and enter a cathedral for viewing artwork. Rome has dozens of Catholic churches and I visited many of them. I had the opportunity to see the "Pieta" up close, before it was damage by a vandal and caged so you can't get that close any longer. I strained my neck with all the other tourists to experience Michelangelo's Sistine Chapel in Vatican City. I wondered at the survival of the original painting of "The Last Supper," and wish I had seen it after it was cleaned instead of before. I marveled at the photographs of the building housing "The Last Supper" where three of four walls were bombed out or partially destroyed and the wall with the painting still stood.

I also had the opportunity to smell the canals in Venice and experiece the pidgeons in the piazza. I cocked my head to straighten up the Leaning Tower of Pisa. I watched the bears perform in the Bern "bear pits." I stood at the very tip top of the Zugspitz and looked down on the tops of other mountains (a strange feeling with your feet firmly planted on the ground and a scene I had only experienced in an airplane). I visited a country so small the train stops in Austria and you have to walk over the border (Lichtenstein). I attended an opera written by an Italian about Japanese culture sung in German (*Madam Butterfly*), and reveled in more feasts for all my senses than I possibly have time to describe.

The Air Force didn't send me to Germany for an art and pleasure tour, but I got one anyway. It was a wonderful education and without question, it created an appreciation for good, classical art which has stayed with me the rest of my life.

28

An Off the Base Discovery

I was wandering around the city of Munich on my own one day and came across a little neighborhood "bar" called the Stockelschwine, which I was told was German for the Porcupine. The equivalent to this establishment in the U. S. might be more like a roadside inn or tavern. There was a small bar in an alcove at the right as you entered the front door. But there were also eight or ten tables to the left. They served beer and other alcoholic drinks, but you could also order food from a limited menu. There was no dance floor and no music, but on Friday and Saturday nights there was "entertainment".

I discovered this bar on a Saturday evening and was delighted to find I was the only American in the place. I got a few strange looks from patrons, even though I was dressed in civilian clothes and not obviously military. But the cute, young, German woman behind the bar smiled at me and I sat down at the bar and ordered a beer.

Her name was Ruth and over the next year or so until I no longer had my own transportation, we actually became reasonably good acquaintances. I would have liked more, but it was not to be.

Around nine o'clock that first evening a very large easel with paper eight feet long and four feet high, was rolled out from the back and placed along the wall. The "entertainment" was a German who was a quick sketch artist. He would tell a story and, as he was telling it, he would sketch the story on the paper. He worked rapidly and in large format and a picture would roll out from his hand in very short order. He was very personable, even though I had no idea what he was saying as I didn't speak German. However his audience seemed to enjoy whatever story he was telling, which appeared to be humorous. He told stories and sketched for about an hour.

By midnight, and time for me to head back to base, I was thoroughly enchanted with The Stockelswine and Ruth. I was determined to find my way back the following Saturday night. This was the time period after Gloria had left and I had no reason to stay at the base. The very fact there were no other Americans there appealed to me.

Over the next few months I visited The Stockelschwine most Saturday evenings, never once seeing an American enter, and became friendly with many of the regulars, as well as Ruth. Even though by now the Germans there knew I was stationed at the Air Base, after a while they either forgot or didn't care. I got into the habit of closing the bar when I was there, and sometimes Ruth would cook me a meal after. She'd take me back to the kitchen and fry up wiener schnitzel and potatos, and watch me eat. I always offered to pay for a meal for her too, but she never accepted. She knew I was taken with her, and although she discouraged me, she was kind.

One evening when I entered and took my regular seat at the bar, a woman who I thought of as "older" moved over and sat down on the stool beside me. She introduced herself in English and we got to talking. Soon she mentioned Ruth, and told me Ruth was her "girl." I interpreted that to mean she was telling me to leave Ruth alone. She left shortly thereafter. I don't believe Ruth was a lesbian or that this woman was really her lover. I never got those vibes. What I do believe is that Ruth put a friend up to saying what she did just to get me to back off a bit, which I did. I still went to the bar and Ruth still was as friendly as ever. I just never again suggested in word or action what relationship I would have liked with her. It didn't really matter whether Ruth was a lesbian or not, she found a gentle way to let me know she wasn't interested without blowing me off. After all, I was a regular paying customer.

One of the good things about Germany while I was stationed there in 1953-55 was that I never needed to learn the language as most Germans could speak English, or at least enough to carry on a decent conversation. English was a required subject in the equivalent of our elementary school. At that time, many young German boys and girls only went to school until age fourteen, when they then apprenticed out to some chosen occupation. Only the "better" families continued their education and considered university. Remember, this was less than ten years after the end of WWII.

Another time I entered the Stockelschwine on my usual Saturday and ordered my regular beer. I turned around on my stool to look over the patrons for this evening and my eye caught the attention of a pretty, zaftig blond woman at a table with two men. We smiled at each other. A little later she came over to me at the bar and asked if I wanted to join them at the table, which I did. The blond's name was Greta and she was thirtyish. Somewhere along the line she asked if I had a car. I told her I did. She took hold of my upper arm and told me she wanted me to take her home. I'm sure I did a double take, but considered this a surprising turn of events. It got even more surprising! First, she told me pointing to one of the men, we had to drop her husband off at a friend's house so he could spend the night there!

The three of us piled into my Ford Taurus and she directed me through Munich and we dropped her husband off in front of a house. Then she pointed me toward her apartment. My knowledge of the streets of Munich was only minimal and before we were stopped at her place, I was pretty well lost as far as directions go.

We spent a couple of hours making love, but remember, I wasn't really all that knowledgeable having made love to only two women at this point in my life. Although I did apparently sexually satisfy her with my limited comprehension of love making, she did mention towards the end she thought I'd be more experienced. I had not yet practiced cunnilingus and suspect that was what she expected.

When I left her apartment about three in the morning, I had no idea which way to drive to get back to Erding, and there weren't many people walking the streets at that time of the night to ask! I drove around a while and finally found a man standing on a corner. I stopped and asked directions to Erding, but he didn't seem to understand me. I knew the road I needed went past the airport, so I simply said, "Flughaven?" That he understood and pointed in the general direction. I stopped two more people that early morn for directions to the airport and finally found the road I needed that got me back to base.

The last night I visited the Stockelschwine I stayed to closing, didn't eat anything, and was a bit intoxicated when I left. I didn't usually drink much simply because I didn't like the taste of beer, didn't like how it made me feel, and couldn't afford to drink anyway. Back then you got paid very little as an enlisted person, although the favorable exchange rate of Dollars to Marks helped (about one to five then). Unfortunately, I was not in a condition I should have been driving at all. About half way to the base I slightly missed a curve, side-swiped a tree and flipped my Taurus on its side. As the car slid along I could see sparks flashing under the dash. Despite my condition, I thought of fire and when the car come to a halt I used the heel of my hand to knock out the windshield, which had loosened in the crash. I crawled out of the car as quickly as possible, but there wasn't any fire.

Along the highways in the countryside are situated small villages, or really clusters of the houses of farmers where their fields stretched out from the burgh. I conveniently had flipped my car just at the edge of one of these villages, and the noise woke up the occupants. I had a few minor cuts on my wrist and one of the farm wives took me into her house to attend to them. No one in this small accumulation of a dozen houses or so could speak

English. It was at this time I realized that, although I could not really speak German, I knew enough words to be able to communicate what happened and ask for a telephone to call the Air Base.

Yes, there was a telephone, one telephone. Someone went and woke up the person who owned the shop that had the telephone, and he let me in to call Erding Air Base. In an hour or so, a base tow truck showed up with two guys. I had told them I wasn't hurt, so no medical people were sent. They boosted my car upright and hooked it up to the tow truck as I went around thanking everybody for taking care of me. The two airmen stuck me in the cab seat between them and headed back to the base. They asked me, and I agreed, to drop the car at a civilian repair station, and they took me into the base.

The shock of having the accident, and the two hours plus it took for the tow truck to pick me up and take me back to base, must have sobered me up. Even though I had to make a report when I got back, no one even asked me if I had been drinking. I found out later that if the question had come up, I could have been court marshaled (again). Eventually the car was repaired, although never the same. By the time it was fixed, a couple of new, interesting women had arrived at the base, and I never went back to the Stockelschwine. When I shipped back home, I left my car with one of the new "friends" in Germany to sell and send me the proceeds. A few months later I got a note from her telling me she had lost the vehicle in a poker game. She did say she was sorry.

29

The Rest of My Air Frce Tour

One day I got notice that two new women were coming to our base and I was to meet them at the Munich train station. That was standard procedure. There was no easy way to get from Munich to the Erding Air Base unless you knew there was a local train between the two cities. So whenever there were new women arriving, as the First Sergeant I would order a car or bus with a driver and go meet them in Munich.

The women had been on the train from Frankfurt to Munich just like I had done a couple of years previous. The were both in their mid-twenties. Pat was white, the other woman was black. She told me to call her Bugs, as that was her nickname. We talked on the drive back to Erding about the base, our unit, their jobs, our wonderful women's bar and anything else I could think of to get them acquainted with being stationed in Germany. It seemed to me they both stared at me the whole trip, but I put it down to their listening carefully to me expound.

I write about this memory because it turns out both of them caught on immediately to my being a lesbian. In the long run I ended up bedding each of them, at separate times, and Bugs taught me the joy of cunnilingus. I hadn't realized I was that obvious as a lesbian when I was just being myself, but fortunately nothing negative ever came of it.

Finally the day came when my time was up in the Air Force, and I received orders to ship home for discharge. Before I could leave, I had to have final evaluations from both my immediate Captain in charge of the women's barrack, and the Adjutant of my general unit. The highest rating was superior, but for some reason, the rules were such that you could not get both evaluations at that level. My Adjutant came first and gave me the superior rating. From his point of view I did my job well and never gotten into trouble. When it came time for the second evaluation from my Captain, she explained she could only give me an above average rating because of the rules. She and I had some history together (not sexually, although I wouldn't have minded). She knew I was a lesbian and a rebel, and she seemed apologetic about the less than perfect rating. She signed the form, looked up at me and said, "After all, you *are* efficient!"

I traveled back to Frankfurt am Main to await a flight back to the U. S. The military in charge of all people of all services and the diplomatic corp put us up together in a hotel, two to a room. My roommate, Andrea, was a twenty-one year old woman who had been teaching American servicemen's children in an elementary school in Saudi Arabia. She had graduated from high school at sixteen, and from college at nineteen and immediately had taken the Saudi job. She was married to a soldier still stationed in Saudi Arabia, and she was returning to the states because she had been accepted to Columbia School of Medicine in New York.

We kicked around the hotel for three days waiting for seats back to the U.S. We finally got the call and went to the room to pack up what few things we had at the hotel. Andrea was a smoker. As we were just about to leave the room, she took out a cigarette and lighter and I reached over, took the lighter out of her hand and flicked it to light her cigarette. Very butch. We gaze into each other's eyes and my thought was I'd just blown three days and *now* we're headed for an airplane.

I was wet for the twenty four hours of the flight: Frankfurt to Scotland to Greenland to New York. Remember, no passenger jets at that time. I sat next to her, touched her when possible without objection from her and sweated the time. When we finally touched down I headed for the Air Base in Brooklyn and she went home. However, she had given me her telephone number when we parted. It took a week to get separated from the Air Force. I called Andrea in New York when I knew what day my discharge was coming through. She had started medical school on the Monday after we arrived. I was discharged on Friday and took a taxi into New York.

I was discharged with only my uniform to wear back home. When the cabby pulled up in front of the address she had given me, he looked around the neighborhood and my uniform and asked, "Are you sure to want to come here?" I checked the address and told him yes. When I rang the doorbell I was greeted by Andrea's mother who was expecting me and led me up a staircase to the second floor. Andrea wasn't home from school yet, but her parents were. I spent a nervous, but interesting, hour or so talking with them. I notice a lot of books on engineering on the shelves, asked if he was a engineer and got a long story about his building bridges in Germany before WWII. Apparently from his story, when Hitler came into power and he fled the country, he also blew up a bridge or two behind him! Interesting guy!

Andrea eventually arrived home and we had only a few minutes together before dinner. When I kissed her, she kissed back. She told me she had reserved a room for me at the Commodore Hotel, significantly fancier and more expensive than I had ever experienced before. After dinner with her parents, she drove me over there, kissed me goodnight and said the next day, Saturday, she had to go to school in the morning, but would be available in the afternoon.

On Saturday Andrea took me to the Empire State Building. Even though she was a native New Yorker, she said she had never been there herself so it was new. We did some other sightseeing and then went back to my hotel. After dinner we went to my very small single room, and spent the better part of the evening making love.

I had made reservations for a flight home the next day and headed back to California. I always wondered if Andrea became the psychiatrist she was aiming for, what she did with her husband, and how she reconciled the one night we had together.

PART 4

LIFE POST MILITARY

30

Arriving Back Home After Four Years

After nearly four years away, I arrived back home in Pasadena on a Sunday. I stayed with my parents as I had practically no clothes other than my uniform and undies, no place to go, and a few hundred dollars with which I was mustered out of the military. As it turned out, I lived with my parents about six months.

The next day I hightailed it down to Pasadena City College to see if I could sign up for classes as the semester had just begun. I went in my uniform and was told no, I was too late as registration had closed the previous Friday. I argued I had been in New York, still serving my country on Friday and couldn't they make an exception as classes had only started that day. Nope, they said, no exceptions.

So I forgot about school at that time and decided I needed a job. I called my favorite teacher from elementary and high school, to let her know I was back from my military service, not even wondering whether or not she cared one way or the other. However that contact led to my first job. Her husband was working for a very small company making modeling clay and several modeling kits for retail sales, mostly under another company's name. He offered me a job in Los Angeles, for not very much money, and I learned more than I ever wanted to know about creating modeling clay.

As the owner of the company came into the office every afternoon, pulled out a bottle of liquor and spent three or four hours drinking, that job didn't last very long, about three months or so when it essentially went out of business. I started looking for a new occupation. I had no work history except in military supply and a few months of creating modeling clay. Neither of those were going to get me a job. I interviewed with the telephone company. I was honest and told my interviewer I didn't know if I was going to stay a civilian or reenlist in the Air Force. She said if I decided not to reenlist, come back and see her, but meanwhile, no job as they didn't wanted to invest in training me just to have me leave in a short while. So much for honesty.

I didn't know much about job hunting, never having done so before, and ended up with an employment agency who placed me, for a fee, with a jewelry stones and findings company in Pasadena. There I learned more than I ever wanted to know about jewelry parts, and how to count and package them. I lasted a few months there until they realized I was a lesbian and didn't fit in with their far right philosophy. It particularly upset them that I was throwing passes at the bosses' daughter, who also worked there. I was given a choice of quitting or being fired. Under the circumstances, I thought that was kind of them. This was the first, last, and only time I was fired for being a lesbian. So much for paying to get employment.

Job hunting again. This time I spotted an ad in the local classifieds in the fledgling electronics industry. Got the job and learned all I ever wanted to know about winding and finishing transformer coils. Boring. However the company got sold to William Miller Instruments and I went along for the ride. Things started to pick up and I received training in wiring medical equipment. I got so good at it, I eventually had the opportunity to wire prototypes. WMI then got sold to Kodak within two years of my getting the original job. It was an interesting experience to work for three companies without actually changing jobs.

At the jewelry findings company I experienced my first job discrimination; at Kodak I found my second. I sat along side men who were doing exactly the same job I was. In some cases, I was doing it better. But we didn't get the same pay; I got less. Frankly I wasn't concerned about the political aspects at that time, only my shorter paycheck for more and/or better work. It didn't seem fair. Even at that young age of twenty three, fair was important to me. I asked for a raise, pointing out my observations. I had become good acquaintances with my immediate supervisor and knew I could talk to him. Not that it mattered as he didn't have jurisdiction on pay raises. However he did bring the subject up with management and was appropriately chagrined when he explained to me the answer was no raise. Why? Because I was a single woman, and the man to whom I was comparing myself, who I wouldn't have hired at all, was married with two children. Yep, management had the audacity to actually say that! Consider the time period.

By now I was no longer living at home and had started to think about going back to school. As it turned out I worked for this three-in-one company about three years and then, after I quit to attend college, my supervisor friend hired me back short time over the two following summers to earn money to go back to classes in the fall. I told you, he was pretty hep, even if his hobby was roller dancing with his wife.

31

Virginia and Back to School

My mother was a religious person, I think. I say it that way because, since the time I can remember, she nearly always went to her Methodist church on Sunday and the women's circle one Wednesday a month. When I was a child I sometimes went with her to the Circle Picnic. But the fact is my mother never talked about religion and I never knew what was in her mind. Maybe she believed and maybe she just found a way to get out of the house. Occasionally my father, who was not religious at all and was probably the reason she never spoke of her faith, drove her to church and someone else brought her home. If no other way to get to church appeared, she would take the bus, but she *always* went.

After I returned from the Air Force and was living at home, I would occasionally go to church with her on Sunday. I had learned in the Air Force I really didn't care for religion, particularly Christianity, but driving my mom to church once in a while seemed a nice thing to do. Despite my continued dislike of her, I was living in her house.

One Sunday soon after my return home, I took one look at the choir, my jaw dropped and my stomach started rumbling in that fashion that declares you are very attracted to the person you're looking at. I asked my mother who was the women in the second row, fourth from our right. She told me her name was "Mrs ...." whose first name was also Virginia, the same as my sister. I watched Virginia from the audience a couple of weeks and the butterflies continued. I was determined I was going to meet her. I could only find one way to do it; I joined the choir!

Could I sing? Not very well! I don't know about other church choirs, but this one never refused anyone. Apparently it was the Christian way of doing things in their institution. Virginia sang lead; I sang lead. At an early practice,

I suggested to the choir director maybe I could sit next to Virginia and follow her lead. It took very little time to get acquainted.

I finally got up enough nerve and asked Virginia out to dinner, and she accepted. After dinner I drove her home and, instead of stopping at her house, I drove right past, pulled up to the curb and kissed her. She absolutely did not react one iota. I pulled back, looked at her blank face and circled the block to drop her off at her home, only saying good night.

Being young and full of myself, I remembered later that even though she hadn't reacted to my attempted kiss, she hadn't pushed me away or said anything negative either. So the next evening I stopped by her house unannounced. After a while of following her around the house, I backed her into a corner in the kitchen and tried the kiss again. This time she reacted and kissed me back. She acknowledged how difficult it had been the previous evening not to react to my kiss, and off to bed we went.

My mother did not understand why I was going to move in with the lady from the church choir. It was another ten years before my mother and I actually spoke about my sexual orientation.

Virginia was taller than me, five foot, seven, with long black hair she would wear as a bun when going to work. She was thirteen years older and was actually married at the time, although her husband was not in the country when we met. I was the first women lover in her life. She worked in the insurance department of a large corporate company, but unfortunately had the propensity of being late to work every day. No matter how hard she tried, or how early she got up, it was not in her nature to arrive to work on time. The good news was she never got fired for it, at least while I knew her. She told me that when she was younger she had worked as a prostitute in a house in Seattle (which was where she met her husband), but had given that up after a few years. She certainly had the looks for it, and didn't appear to have any emotional scars from the experience

I lived five years with Virginia. The first two were wonderful, including her teaching me to dance a little. The second couple of years weren't so good while we dealt with her homophobia, our association with a singing group named Sweet Adelines and her sister who lived next door. Yes, sister, her husband and two kids lived next door and their mother frequently visited the sister, but never us.

During this period Virginia's husband came back from Alaska where he had been working as a furniture mover. He was somewhat confused there was someone else sleeping in his bed. A very butch looking woman at that! Virginia filed for divorce (she had been contemplating that anyway), and he slept on the couch until he got himself a new job and a place to stay.

Meanwhile in the third year of our relationship we talked about my starting college. I was eligible for the GI Bill which would help pay for my education. It paid $110.00 a month! Even in the late 1950's that was not enough to do much more than buy your books and provide some food. But Virginia was determined I would go back to school, and she supported me for two years by taking just my GI money for room and board and any other needs. To this day I'm not sure I would have started college before the opportunity to do so expired, except for Virginia's urging.

I started my education by returning to Pasadena City College where I actually had a head start. When I was in senior high, the last two years of high school and the first two of college were combined in what was called Pasadena Junior College. As an outstanding high school student, I had been allowed to take a couple of college courses while still in the twelfth grade. Besides those units, the school awarded me four units of military science. Thus I was able to complete the first two years of college in one and a half years, at which time I transferred to UCLA.

Unfortunately, Virginia just couldn't handle being a lesbian. She was afraid of what people would think of her. She was scared anyone visiting would realize there was only one bedroom with one bed. She started drinking more heavily, going out on her own, and going back to men. I took it for a while, not knowing where she was some nights or when she would be home. Sometimes it wasn't until morning and I knew she was sleeping with someone who wasn't a woman. I felt I couldn't compete with the legitimacy of any male.

I went about finding a small, "bachelor" apartment with no cooking facilities in West Los Angeles near UCLA, and moved out of Virginia's house and life. I still had my GI Bill and some money I had made during the summer which got me started.

I then went about looking for some kind of work on campus and ended up being a subject in a smog research project. We were being tested for sensitivity to the chemical components of local "smog." At this point we were drawing near the end of the semester. It turned out I was a very reliable subject and the professor conducting the research asked me if I could stay and work with her during the summer. I told her no, that I had a summer job in the electronics industry, and it was necessary for me to work during the off season in order to have money enough to come back to school in the fall.

She asked me if I would work with her instead if she could find me a job on campus that would take up the rest of the summer. I told her sure, not thinking it would ever come about. A few days later she gave me the name of a person to go see for a possible job.

I hiked over to an old wooden building in the Engineering Department compound at UCLA. The sign in front said Institute of Transportation and Traffic Engineering. I had no idea what that meant. Turns out it was research in human engineering, meaning engineering roads, cars, signs–anything having to do with traffic–to fit the human driver, a new concept for auto makers and highway designers.

I was shown about the facilities, particularly the Driving Simulation Laboratory. About an hour later my interviewer said, "Well?" I said, "Well, what?" He said, "Do you want the job?" I said, "That's it?" He said, "You came well recommended." I said, "OK."

I got smogged some more during the summer and then spent the next twenty years in Research in Traffic Safety, thanks to Virginia's early willingness to support me in education, if not in love.

32

The Institute of Transportation and Traffic Engineering

My major in college was psychology. Don't ask me what I intended to do with that when I graduated, because I couldn't possibly tell you. But in the way that things tend to turn out perfect, most of what you learn in undergraduate psychology classes relates to experimental psychology, not clinical psychology. What I was hired to work on at ITTE was related to testing humans in the Driving Simulation Laboratory and other research projects having to do with human reactions to the driving experience.

This can also be referred to as experimental psychology, which in our research was called human engineering.

Over the eighteen years I worked at UCLA ITTE, our research covered such projects as driving in a sleep deprived state, testing signs for interchanges, driving under the influence of alcohol and other drugs (including marijuana), testing knowledge of pavement striping and markings, testing the visibility of reflectorized bicycle tires, and other projects. I spent fifteen years working on the problem of the wrong way driver and did the initial research on the signs you now see at the bottom of freeway off ramps warning drivers they are about to go the wrong way up an off ramp. My last research project, which you can also see in the real world every day you drive the Los Angeles freeways, is the use and wording of the changeable message boards on interstate highways.

I graduated with a bachelor's degree a couple of years after beginning to work at ITTE, and was offered a full time job. I soon became the supervisor of the Driving Simulation Laboratory. The Laboratory consisted of a real car with a real engine which drove the rear wheels on rollers activating motion picture projectors that cast an image on all four sides of the car.

At the time we were the most sophisticated driving simulation laboratory in the world, and we would frequently get visitors from other countries to view our simulator, ride in it, and ask questions. I understand after seeing ours, the representatives from Japan went home and built one of their own patterned after our simulator. All simulators now, flight and otherwise, use video presentations. They didn't exist back then.

We created our own motion pictures using a special camera car with cameras on all four sides capturing a 360 degree image. For various projects we created films on freeways, city streets and country roads. I learned a lot about the making of motion pictures and assisted the professional cameraman we hired when we went on location. It was frequently my job to load the rear camera which pointed backwards to capture the image in the rear view mirror in the simulator.

By necessity, I learned a lot about editing motion pictures as we spliced together miles and miles of highway to create a non-stop drive for the simulator. For some projects, like testing sleep deprived subjects, we had them drive for a couple of hours, or to the point they fell asleep at the wheel, whichever came first.

Because of my acquired knowledge of motion picture photography and editing, I once created a one minute stop-action motion picture of cars driving both ways on the freeway with *green* running lights in the rear–a concept that was being considered for all automobiles, but was not adopted. At twenty-four frames per second, it takes 1,440 frames, shot one at a time, to create a one minute stop action film! I built a toy-sized highway myself and wired miniature toy cars with headlights, taillights, and brake lights using colored "grain of wheat" light bulbs. The finished product looked pretty good, even if I do say so myself, with several cars, going both ways on a four lane highway, and at different speeds. Just like the real world.

As far as the Driving Simulation Laboratory is concerned, we had the driver and the car itself wired to record analog data. The UCLA School of Engineering housed one of a very few number (I believe two or three in the whole United States) of analog computers. This one was called SWAC (South West Analog Computer), and was one of the very earliest of computers. This computer was the size of a room, literally, and had less computing power than that of a modern cell phone. But we either analyzed the collected data through SWAC or tediously by hand from analog graphs created when the Simulator was operating.

I could probably write a book by itself on the research I worked on at UCLA, but I'm not going to. Suffice it to say that every year was a different grant and a different project; it was extremely difficult to get bored. It was the best kind of a job anyone could ask for, except occasionally for the hours.

In most cases the hours were normal, but when it was a special project which required a twenty four hour run on the Simulator, or testing subjects in their ability to see bicycle tires at night after dark, or out on the road for 12-14 hour days shooting film, that's what we did. No overtime, no union, and no regrets.

There also was a significant amount of freedom, so long as we met deadlines and finished the project on time. One day in January, Southern California was experiencing a heat wave. It was in the eighties and too nice to be indoors. As supervisor, I closed the office for the afternoon and we all went to the beach! That's what I call freedom on the job.

When I began to work at ITTE there were about eighty people in the Institute. However, after the environment became the hot "cause of the year," interest in keeping people from killing themselves on the highway went out of style and grants for research in traffic safety began to slack off. Slowly the staff dwindled as projects shut down. Then our parent Institute, which was located on the Berkeley Campus, closed down the UCLA off-shoot. You know the old saying "will the last one out please turn off the lights"? That was me! No way could I have predicted eighteen years earlier I would be the last to go. I spent the last couple of months after being laid off finishing the report on my final project, the changeable message boards, without pay.

I couldn't walk away without completing the commitment, which should tell you tons about me.

33

Early Bar Experiences

You go back a long way in Los Angeles if you can remember the earliest of bars, the If Club and the Open Door. Both of them were downtown, although I can't remember at this point what street they were on. I do remember they weren't too far away from each other.

The important thing to consider is this: at that time in history (mid-1950s) it was illegal to even be a lesbian, let alone be one out in public displaying your sexuality. But you still wanted to know there were others like you who didn't fit into the heterosexual world that you despised. I'm speaking for myself, of course, but I also know many, if not most, other lesbians felt the same way. If we knew any other lesbians, we met in private homes. We wanted more than that.

I went to the If Club only once, but several times to the Open Door. It was named well as the door was, literally, open to everyone. If you entered this bar, you knew in advance you were going to be on display for heterosexual couples who came to look at the lesbians. It wasn't a pleasant situation, but it was what was available.

A bit later I visited a bar whose name I cannot remember, but whose atmosphere was very different. It was the first bar I remember which was filled with lesbians and few or no "tourists." There was a jukebox and dancing! You weren't allowed to touch your partner, and sometimes the police would come around to be sure you were not doing so. But there were some women that could dance in the sexiest way I had ever seen without touching! It was enough to turn you on, and those who were not capable of dancing like that, me, for example, still appreciated watching. My memory was that this was a Saturday night only type of club.

Then came the Canyon Club located up in the hills off Topanga Canyon. I never actually attended that club myself, but understand it was mostly for the boys with one night a week for women-only.

About that same time the Rob Roy opened down in the Culver City area and now there was a real place for lesbians. It was a great improvement over any other place I knew for lesbians to gather. A bar, a small dance floor, a jukebox, a patio, and at least in the beginning, served food. Maybe there was a pool? I vaguely remember that was the reason for the patio, but I could be wrong. I was at the Rob Roy several times when the police walked through, which they did on a regular basis. I was never hassled by them. Mostly they were looking for women under twenty one, over intoxicated, or the smell of marijuana. I didn't fit any of those profiles, but they still made me uncomfortable.

There were other not-so-elegant lesbian bars beginning to pop up in the San Fernando Valley and West Hollywood. Most were dark, loud, smoky, served beer and sometimes wine only, and didn't fit my tastes too well. Most lesbian bars back then were owned by strait males.

One exception to that was Joanie Presents, a "night club" on north Lankershim Blvd. By then I was in my motorcycle period and used to ride my bike out there from Culver City where I resided. I rode a red Honda 250 with black accoutrements. It had a windshield and saddle boxes. I wore custom made black leather pants and jacket with red trim, a pair of black engineer boots, and dark glasses. I was single at the time. Joanie Presents was owned and run by Joanie, who had been a drummer in an "all-girls" band during the war. She would star as the live entertainment with two or three other musicians. This lesbian bar was nicely appointed, and much quieter than most places (except when Joanie was drumming).

There was a period of about ten years where lesbian bars were popping up everywhere. They would hang around for a few years and go out of business. It was difficult to get enough women out to each of the many bars to keep them financially stable.

However, I must tell you about a personal experience I once had in a very small bar on Ventura Blvd owned by Miss Beverly Shaw, Sir, an ex-movie actress who appeared to me to be in her sixties. The room consisted of one long bar down the right side as you entered, and not much else. I was sitting about half way along the bar one night sipping a beer. Please note, I didn't like the taste of beer and could make one last a long, long time, but I hadn't yet reached that enlightened time of my life when I could walk in a bar and order a soft drink.

As I and about thirty other lesbians were attending at the bar, two police officers walked in and sauntered down to the far end where Miss Beverly

Shaw, Sir, was leaning on the bar. All eyes followed and watch. After speaking to the police for a few moments, she slowly made her way up behind the bar and stopped right in front of me. She looked at me and asked to see my driver's license, which I promptly pulled out of my pocket. I was in my early thirties at that point and certainly wasn't worried about being busted. Miss Shaw leaned back to read my ID in the light behind the bar and then in a raised, whiskey drinking/cigarette smoking voice, dramatically said, "My God...You're older than I am!" Everybody in the bar burst out laughing as I obviously wasn't older than she was. She smiled at me, returned my license, and casually sauntered back to the far end of the bar. The police officers left immediately thereafter.

This is not meant to be a comprehensive compilation of lesbian bars in the Los Angeles area. It is only the ones I frequented in the years between my early twenties and early-thirties. The fact is, I was never a "bar person." I didn't like the taste of alcohol or what it did to me. I still don't.

34

The Air Force Reserve

I spent a few months short of four years in the regular Air Force. Soon after my job interview with the telephone company, I decided I wouldn't re-up in the Air Force, but I would, and did, join the active AF Reserves. I spent the next twelve years in the active reserve, one weekend a month and two weeks in the summer on duty in uniform.

I started out stationed (for the monthly weekends) in Long Beach, was moved to March AFB in Riverside and ended up at Lompoc's Vandenburg AFB. I knew supply, so I was in supply, specifically in a medical field unit like the one you saw in M*A*S*H. In our case, however, the field "hospital" was all in boxes in case we needed to be activated and shipped in an emergency to an active war location.

The unit consisted of administrative officers, doctors, nurses, other medical personnel, and non-medical support staff such as myself. Some of the people had served time on active duty and were gathering additional years toward retirement. Most of the male personnel, medical and enlisted , were getting out of serving in the military by doing six weeks on active duty and four years in the active reserve. Occasionally you'd even have a celebrity in your unit. We had singer Jack Jones and actor Max Bauer. Very different personalities.

Mostly the reserve time was pretty boring, but it had its moments. I will always remember the two weeks we spent our summer training at Lackland AFB in San Antonio, Texas when the temperature never fell below ninety degrees at night. Daytime was above one hundred ten degrees. Just try to keep your heavily starched cotton uniform from wilting in that kind of heat.

One tour of duty, in Mountain Home, Idaho, we received a notice some of us could take a flight in a refueling plane on a training exercise. Pilots doing their two week tour were always our pilots to and from our destinations as they had to train just like we did. I showed up at the flight line with three guys. The pilot lined us up and stood in front of the four of us. He pointed at the men one by one and said,"You can't go, you can't go, you can't go." He pointed at me and said, "You can go." All three men were dressed in their Class A uniforms. I was dressed in my fatigues and boots, proper clothing for flying in a military aircraft. There is an unwritten rule about flying in the Air Force: you don't go up in a plane unless you're dressed to walk back.

We took off: two pilots, a refueling sergeant, and me. Our mission was to refuel a jet in mid-air. You do that by dropping a snorkel down to the plane flying below you and poking it into a small intake valve at the front top of the jet. You lay on your belly, sighting down the snorkel. The sergeant told me if all went well, he'd give me a chance to try it. From where I was watching, that valve hole looked about the size of a pencil eraser!

About the time the jet had eased up below and behind us and the fuel snorkel was down and searching to connect with the intake valve, our four-engine aircraft "lost" an engine, meaning it stopped working. The pilot "feathered" the opposing engine (shut it down) to balance power, and the refueling exercise was quickly terminated. The sergeant said, "Sorry, kid." We had no problem getting back to the airfield with two engines over miles and miles of sagebrush, and I didn't end up having to walk back, even if I was dressed for it. Nevertheless, it was a fascinating experience I'll never forget.

There were about one thousand enlisted personnel in my reserve unit. Each year the administrative officers would pick one airman who the officers considered an outstanding person and declare him/her "Airman of the Year" for that unit. I was chosen one year out of all those guys. It wasn't a big deal in the unit, but the information was submitted to the newspaper in my home town as a matter of procedure. For me, that was the *Pasadena Star News*. It so happened the performance at the Pasadena Play House running at that time was "No Time for Sergeants" with Andy Griffith in the lead role. Some editor at the *Star News* picked up on that and contacted the Play House. Not only did I get written up in the newspaper, but I was invited to be guest of honor at a performance of the play. It all connected you see, and I got my fifteen minutes of fame.

In order to receive any retirement benefits from the military, you must serve twenty "good" years. I quit with sixteen years to my credit, four short of any benefits. Why? Because I was no longer the same person and the U.S. was engaged in the war in Viet Nam, which I did not believe in. I fully understood what I was doing, and I could no longer support the military. I knew I would forfeit any retirement and it didn't matter. I've been asked if I couldn't have hung in for four more years and then quit. The answer is no. If I had to make the choice again, it would be the same.

I'm proud of my service time and left the Air Force as a Master Sergeant (six stripes). Both my regular service and reserve service discharges are honorable, even though the last officer I worked for knew I was a lesbian, and simply didn't care.

35

Sherry

I met Sherry in the Rob Roy one night and instantly fell in love. I was single and sharing an apartment with a friend. Sherry was not single. We got to talking and when she excused herself to go to the restroom, I followed her in. When she had finished and was heading toward the door I stepped in front of her, put my arms around her and kissed her.

I fell in love with Virginia instantly when seeing her from a distance. I fell in love with Sherry instantly having a conversation with her in a bar. I think there was a pattern going here, and in retrospect, I believe I fell in lust, not love. However, like a fairly typical lesbian couple, Sherry dumped her partner, my roommate moved elsewhere, Sherry moved in, and we set up housekeeping together.

At that time, Sherry was a receptionist, a job well below the level she was capable of. I was full time at UCLA, and it seemed logical to me to offer her a better job than she had, so I hired her. I had three or four other women, and sometimes work study students in my department, and Sherry was a great addition to my work force.

Everybody liked Sherry; she was cute with curly short hair, a nice smile, large bosoms, and a great personality. What's not to like? Remember earlier I mentioned a falling out with my sister Anne over one of my lovers who she didn't care for? That was Sherry. It all stemmed from a time we were visiting Anne and Sherry made herself at home and opened Anne's refrigerator looking for something to eat. A tiny incident my sister took exception to and which cost Anne and I a falling out for five years, although Sherry's and my relationship only lasted two years. On the other hand, my boss and his wife like Sherry so well they would come to dinner at our house like any other married couple.

By now the Engineering Department had purchased a new IBM 360, one of the early digital computers. As it turned out, Sherry had an interest in learning to work with the computer. There was no such thing as a personal computer yet, only huge monsters and if you wanted to work with it, you went to where it lived in its air-conditioned environment. Although Sherry and I were lovers, it was also advantageous to our Laboratory for her to learn computers. So I gave her the opportunity to study and practice on work time. Her aptitude was so great she went on to be a systems programmer for TRW (where I had originally stolen her as their receptionist) and she eventually retired from TransAmerica.

Meanwhile, I was participating in the active Air Force Reserve. Sherry went with me one weekend, and met some of the Airmen and Officers of my unit who instantly fell all over themselves to impress her. They asked her if she would like to join the AF Reserve. At that time there was a requirement that recruits in the Reserve had to take six weeks of Basic Training, then go back to their civilians jobs spending one weekend a month and two weeks in the summer on duty. The men in my unit wanted Sherry so badly they did the unheard of thing of waiving the Basic Training and recruiting her directly into the Reserve! Her commitment was for three years, which she completed even after we'd broken up.

Any break up is emotional. This one was particularly so for me because she left me to "find herself," and she was doing that with men. I didn't feel as if I could compete with the heterosexual world, but more than that, the first two women I attempted to have live-in relationships with, left me for men. Sherry tried being married for a few years and during that period we became friends. I'm happy to say she finally divorced and came back to the lesbian fold and has been happily in a good lesbian relationship for a number of years. More importantly, after forty years, she and I are still friends even though we live too far apart to see each other anymore.

At the time of our breakup it was quite obvious to me there was something wrong with me. Gloria had forgotten about me in less time than it took her ship to cross the sea. Virginia turned away from me and being a lesbian, going back to men and eventually getting married again. Sherry left me to find herself with men and actually married one. Obviously I was inadequate or unable to pick the right kind of women as a partner. Either concept was devastating, and led me to the lowest time in my life.

36

Jo To My Rescue!

Jo and I were never lovers, just the very best of friends. She was my motorcycle buddy and my savior during the lowest period of my life–although I doubt she ever realized it completely. There were also a few times I pulled her ass out of the fire. Jo was the kind of person you rarely meet, but when you do you become instant friends. Even if you're separated by several states and don't see each other for a few years, you still know she'd be there for you, no matter what. The only other person I ever felt that way about was my oldest sister, Anne. They were my two backups in life; the two places I knew I could go if I really needed to. I have lost both of them now, and I miss having that security in my background, even though I might never have used it.

Tall, slim but muscular, and very butch, Jo complained that she could hardly walk down the street without the police stopping and hassling her. She once asked why the police never stopped me, only her. She was an extremely talented woman, having been an interior decorator at one time in her life. She had gotten married as a teenager just to get away from her parents, but I think she knew from the beginning that wasn't going to last. A smoker from an early age, she told me she had been hospitalized a couple of times with lung infections. She passed away much too young with lung cancer.

Jo owned and ran a lesbian bar on Melrose called The Seventh Circle. When it first opened I visited once or twice to check it out. Jo's partner was a belly-dancer and the entertainment. It was a small neighborhood bar which Jo had taken over and encouraged lesbian patrons. By law you cannot block out anyone over twenty one, so there were always a straight guy or two around, but we outnumbered them and kept them in check most of the time.

As I said, Jo and I became instant friends and I learned a new trade: to draw beer. Occasionally when she was short a bartender, I'd go behind the bar and help out. She offered to pay me, but I never accepted because I felt being her employee, even on a limited bases, would change our relationship, and I didn't want to do that. I also learned to play pool which I'd never done before, and eventually became part of The Seventh Circle's team in the pool bar league.

Only once did I get into a confrontation at the bar. A straight neighborhood male punk had come in and was really bothering a woman sitting at the bar. I told him to back off, but he continued. I was rarely in a good mood during that time period of my life; I didn't think, I reacted. I grabbed his shirt and pressed him down to his knees and said a few choice words about getting out of the bar and leaving us the shit alone. He didn't say a word, but when I let go of his shirt, he got up and left. I looked up and Jo was staring at me as if she had seen a ghost. She told me she couldn't believe I'd done that. Not only was it out of character, but, she said, this guy was a bad dude who had just gotten out of jail and she was afraid she was going to have to shoot him to save me (she always had a hand gun under the bar and had reached for it). Personally, I think he was so surprised he was just caught off guard. Although he did come back to the bar, I'm not aware that he ever hassled a women again.

I had a car, but I also had my motorcycle at that time and Jo rode one too. We sometimes rode together, like out to visit other bars (but only Jo had the guts to ride her bike *into* the bar). Once we rode our bikes out to Lake Isabella for a weekend, getting sunburned on the ride out, as well as rained on. We parallel-parked our bikes, threw a blanket over the two of them and called it a "tent." Some guy started target practice near us and we nearly shit in our pants, but the park ranger shut him down pretty quickly. We don't *think* he was trying to scare off two women bikers who looked a bit tough.

At sundown the gnats came out in force, swarming all around our heads. Jo lit up a joint and laughed it off. I didn't smoke. When it got completely dark and we settled down to sleep, field mice started running over the motorcycles and in the tent looking for whatever food they could scrounge. Mice didn't bother me, but they bothered Jo a lot and I doubt she slept all night. We only spent one night camping, and never did it again, but it was fun watching tough Jo being afraid of mice and being willing to let me see it, knowing it would be our secret.

This was a very down period of my life. The lowest I have ever experienced. Poor Jo could never anticipate my mood. I'd get dressed and take myself over to The Seventh Circle, walk in, sometimes say nothing to Jo, turn around, walk right back out again and drive home.

It was in this period I had a probable "breakdown." I was entertaining the worst headache of my life which no over-the-counter medication would touch. I went to Kaiser and saw a doctor who put me on Valium. After a few weeks, I also persuaded the doctor to give me a small prescription for amphetimines. I explained I occasionally needed to take the upper to offset the Valium before driving home. I didn't tell him I already was using small amounts of amphetimines purchased off the street. He said he had probably only written two prescriptions in his life for speed, but he gave me a very limited one for five pills. I had specified exactly what I wanted, and he cooperated, and I never asked him to renew it. It was a subterfuge on my part. What I actually wanted was a prescription I could carry in my wallet to cover the drug I was already buying and using.

After seeing the doctor the first time, I also walked into my boss's office at UCLA and tried to quit my job, even though he wouldn't let me. He told me to take all the time I wanted. After one week he called and said he desperately needed me back and could I come in on Monday. I really resented his saying I could have the time and then calling me back, but I went. It was probably exactly the right thing for him to do. I presumed he'd put me on vacation, but we never actually talked about it.

I spent every hour the bar was open with Jo during that week off from work, and she treated me with kindness, not mentioning anything that was going on with me. That was also probably the best thing, just accepting where I was at without bugging me about it. It was that period that cemented our friendship.

I would never suggest Jo was a druggie, except she did smoke marijuana. One time she tried to grow it in her basement. We set up lights, heat lamps and pots of marijuana seeds and she was supposed to water and take care of them. The experiment didn't turn out too well. Apparently mice like young, tender marijuana shoots which have no chemical potency at all. Every time the tiny plants would pop up out of the soil, the mice would eat them down to the ground! Not to worry, Jo was street smart and knew where to buy anything she needed.

One day I asked Jo to get me some LSD as I had decided I wanted to try it out just to see how it felt. I had attempted to smoke pot, but as I didn't smoke tobacco, I had a difficult time inhaling and it never seem to do anything for me. Jo tried to dissuade me from the LSD, but I told her I wanted just one dose and wasn't interested in anything stronger. I was just curious. In a few days she handed over a wrapped sugar cube, told me to be careful, but said nothing else.

Sherry, my friend and ex, was staying with me at that time. She has stayed with me two or three times in our forty year acquaintance when she was between places to live. The next day, a Saturday, I asked her to take my car keys when she was going out. I explained I was going to take some LSD and didn't want the opportunity to think I was capable of driving. Although she obliged me, I soon realized I would never had considered driving anyway.

I only tried the LSD once, and it really was a truly strange experience. Being me, of course, I went about analyzing each step and condition while I was under the drug. Time did stand still; I had no concept how long all this took except eventually I came down, Sherry came home, and it was much later. But it was the visual aspects that I remember that were the strangest. I have worn glasses since I was about twelve years old. Under the influence of LSD everything was visually magnified and somewhat distorted. Without my glasses I could see the pattern in the bathroom linoleum clear and large. I was fascinated with that and couldn't get over it. I watched some television under the influence of LSD, but couldn't concentrate on the program. Then I went to sleep and when I woke up, I wondered what all the fuss was about. LSD was interesting, but nothing I would consider repeating. I never had a relapse and always wondered if my reaction, or mostly lack of it, was due to the analytic attitude I had while experiencing it.

I've mention several aspects of how Jo was a friend to me, but I was equally a friend to her. On more than one occasion I would receive a telephone call in the middle of the night from her and she would need to be picked up. She'd know where she was, once by the Queen Mary, but she wouldn't have any memory of how she got there. I'd go, pile her into my car and take her back to her home.

There was a time when she had crashed her motorcycle and didn't have any other transportation. Without hesitation I loaned her my bike. When she came to return the bike she was so high on pot she could hardly stand up. She had driven my motorcycle from Highland Park to Culver City, several miles over city streets, telling me that each time she came to a stop at an intersection, she could hardly hold the bike upright.

I have no intent that you should think badly of Jo and I'm defending her because she was my friend. She didn't do hard drugs that I'm aware of, only pot. She didn't get drunk. She was always on time opening the bar and sober when she closed it. She was always a friend when I, or anyone else, needed one. It's very hard for me to condemn her for smoking pot, even though sometimes she worried me. As far as I know, it was her worst indulgence.

After The Seventh Circle closed, she stuck around Los Angeles a few more years in a couple of different occupations, and then she moved back to her home state, Missouri. She bought land out of Noel, which is located in the south-west corner of the state where Missouri, Arkansas and Oklahoma come together. Eventually she built a house, mostly by herself with assistance for the heavy work, and settled down with a woman she had known back in Los Angeles. She seemed to me to be very happy there until the end. I would visit anytime I came near her part of the world, and she would visit me if she came to LA. As I said, I miss this good friend.

37

The Python Incident

I mentioned my love for snakes, maybe related to the one picture of my suicidal brother Roy who was holding a snake. Or maybe not. Before I knew better, I began collecting snakes, both from purchase and some by catching them in the wild. Soon I had a collection of fifteen or so of various varieties: Pythons, King snakes, a wonderful Indigo I got from a UCLA research lab, a Rattlesnake I'd caught in the wild, several species of Boa constrictors, one very poisonous African Gabon Viper (who was not well from the beginning and didn't survive), and a few other varieties that came and went. Needless to say, this was the time period when I wasn't with anyone, or at least not anyone important or for very long.

In December of 1966 I tied a Reticulate Python about six feet long into a gunny sack and put him to soak in the kitchen sink to assist him with shedding his skin. In case you don't know, snakes shed their old skin whenever they grow out of it. Well fed snakes like mine could shed two or three times a year. If the snake is healthy, it usually sheds very easily, sometimes in a single inside-out paper thin slough.

However, this guy was having a bit of trouble. His shed was coming off in pieces and looked messier than I desired. Thinking to aide him by giving him a good soak, I made a mistake. The bag I had placed him in absorbed enough water to close up the weave, disallowing him sufficient air to breath.

I found him later, apparently not breathing, totally limp and, when laid out on the draining board on his back, he remained there and did not attempt to right himself as a snake would generally do. I figured I had nothing to lose by attempting artificial respiration procedures despite the fact I wasn't exactly sure where his lungs were located. This is what I did:

I stretched him out on the draining board on his stomach and straightened him out as much as possible. I check his mouth, but there was no obvious water. He appeared to have swallowed his tongue, but that wasn't important because a snake breathes through his glottis, an opening under the tongue, which was totally retracted. I placed both hands over his back, side by side with my fingers on one side, thumbs on the other, about one third of the distance from the head toward the tail. I gently, but firmly, began retraction and expansion of my fingers, shifting right and then left, until I located the lung area. I determined the latter by the automatic muscular reaction of his jaws upon forced exhalation.

After locating the lung area, I lifted the snake up from his middle, letting his head hang down, in case there was any water to drain out. I continued to squeeze his lung area with the other hand two or three times. No water appeared, so I laid him back out on the draining board and continued squeezing gently at a rate of once every two or three seconds. The first voluntary reaction from the Python was a flicker of his eyeball about thirty seconds later, followed by a brief flick of his tongue. At one point he extruded a few bubbles of air/water from his nostrils. He was breathing sporadically and shallowly, but I continued the artificial respiration procedure at a slower rate. He then began to breath in a "heaving" manner after about three minutes. He rolled his eyeballs occasionally (snakes have no eye lids), and flicked his tongue twice, so I stopped administering pressure and let him rest in the stretched out position, keeping close observation. He made no attempt to move, but after ten minutes or so, his breathing returned to normal and I returned him to his home cage to recover. I monitored him throughout the evening and by morning, about twelve hours after the incident, he appeared normal.

There are two things I don't know: was he really not breathing at all or just so slowly I couldn't detect it, and did he actually have any water in his lungs? A snake's circulation is normally slow, so the lack of oxygen for a few minutes, even ten or fifteen minutes, would not affect him as it would a human being. He appeared to recover completely and grew to about fifteen feet and a radius of seven inches in the following years. He always had a good appetite. Frankly, I'd like to think I saved his life in an heroic manner.

When I was in my low period, I sold all my snakes except one to a dealer. I couldn't let go of the black, mild mannered Indigo with a scar on his side where, while at UCLA, he'd laid under a heat lamp too long and burned himself. It's hard to explain our affection for each other. He was a snake anyone could handle. But no matter who was holding him, he's stretch out toward me one hundred percent of the time. If nothing more, I'm sure he could recognize my scent and associate that with food and comfort. It isn't "love," and it's about all you can expect from an animal with a small, primitive brain, but it's something. He was quite old, and feeding him became a problem. I always fed live mice so as not to waste the food if the snake decided it wasn't hungry. An uneated mouse actually chewed the tip of the tail off the Indigo when I left it in the cage too long. One morning a few months later I rose to find he had died in his sleep. I never regretted selling off the other snakes, and I never regretted keeping the Indigo until he passed naturally.

24 March 2007

My Very Dear Jinx and Kathy,

I'm writing you a joint letter because many of the sentiments contained herein might conceivably interest you both. Or neither of you, but I've got stuff to say, so I beg your forbearances.

First, a News Flash especially for Kathy: Valerie has had her mid-term ultrasound. God help us all, IT'S A BOY. Val Gal was anticipating another little pink princess ballerina, so was speechless with horror. And it's very obvious he ain't gonna be a LITTLE anything. His mother's interim name for his is Thor.

Kathy, thank you so much for getting me *Feminists Who Changed America* for my 150th birthday. It is large, expensive, and impressive. Not to mention a vital part of my Jinx Collection, because it puts her life in context.

I'm chagrinned that it took me sixty years to realize what a profound challenge life is for anyone who deviates in any way from what is considered the "norm". How many times did I brightly chirp at you, Jinx, that sexual orientation is a personal matter and shouldn't affect other aspect of your life?

Well, it SHOULDN'T. And perhaps it didn't in classical Greece, A Midsummer Night's Dream, and Neverland (at least in Michael's version of it).

Then I thought it was a problem only in America. Hadn't the Mother Of Us All (the best historical fiction writer ever), Mary Renault, lived "out" and flourishing in England? A little selective Googling gave me the answer: God, no. She and her lover had to find refuge in South Africa (that bastion of tolerance?) before their neighbors treated them like human beings.

Feminists is chock-full of stories, and no two are alike. They are all empowering, yet there is one aspect that really troubles me: Most of them are obscure, and most educated women are oblivious to them. Only "hard-bitten little chippies" who have miraculously developed respect for their own abilities actually enroll in Women's Studies classes.

Future generations of females, gay and straight, are standing on your shoulders and don't realize it. And what isn't recognized as valuable easily can be torn away. I myself was held captive for a number of years by a faith that demanded I "dumb down" so my husband wouldn't feel "threatened". I thought the ERA was evil. Oh, the wasted years. And the humiliating memories. Some day I hope to forgive myself for all those sweet, dishonest Relief Society lessons I taught to my equally gullible "sisters".

The light started flickering on in my attic over a decade ago. I happened upon a brief biography of that awesome human being, Sojourner Truth. After a couple of paragraphs,

I wondered why every little black girl baby isn't named after her. Then I finished the article, and realized that *every* American girl baby, regardless of "race" (another dubious concept, and another letter) ought to be named Sojourner, to honor her memory.

So all of us, and our progeny, are benefiting from your terrific struggles and sacrifices.

And thank you, Kathy, for sending me the book.

And thank you, Jinx, for being in it.

I love you both and am grateful for your presence in my life.

Love ya,

Gail

P.S. Jinx, I see recent pics of you on the Internet. You look right at home among other writers, scholars, and activists. Perhaps you really *are* home, at last.

38

Wendy: They're Off and Running!

One Christmas season along about 1969 I was invited to go along with a friend to a holiday party at a private residence. Frankly, I'm not much of a party-person, but I went. The residence was the home of two women, Wendy and Pat. Somewhere in the evening I left my phone number with Wendy. Little did I realize the adventure and friendship that would come of that act.

A couple of weeks later I got a phone call at home and the voice on the other end says, "I don't know if you remember me, but ... ." It was Wendy, and of course I remembered her. I was invited over to her and Pat's for the weekend, which turned out to be her family's home. It was raining, but I rode my motorcycle over from Culver City to Altadena anyway. It was a chance to show off my custom made black leathers.

I ended up making love to both Wendy and Pat, separately, not in a threesome, and within a short while they had broken up and Wendy moved in with me. But this memory is not really about our partnership, which only lasted a couple of years, but about our friendship, which now has lasted more than forty years.

I knew nothing about horses and was actually a little afraid of them having only been on one once when I was a teenager. The horse was a whole lot bigger and stronger and, frankly, not within my control. I was in no way harmed, I only was on the back of the animal for a few minutes, but I had and do have a healthy respect for an animal that large. Wendy, however, knew everything about horses, particularly Thoroughbred race horses. She introduced me to the world of Thoroughbred racing, race tracks, horse farms, photography, auctions and Thoroughbred art.

Wendy was, and is, a walking encyclopedia of all things Thoroughbred. She also knows a significant amount about all breeds of horses, Quarter Horses, Jumpers, Arabians and others, but Thoroughbreds are her love. She can cite the lineage of nearly any American horse running for generations back. She knows how each horse in the race should run, in front, from behind or from the middle of the pack until the last furlong where it might thrust forward at the finish with a burst of speed or fade to dead last. Maybe I'm exaggerating; maybe.

The first time Wendy took me to a race, which was at Santa Anita Park, we walked in just as the horses had broken from the gate in a six furlong (three-quarters of a mile) race. It was drizzling and the track was wet. The horses were already out of the gate, about five furlongs to go. The horse running dead last was named "Here Comes Trouble." Wendy looked up, said, "He likes to run in the mud. He ought to win this." He did, flying down the stretch, skimming the wet surface of the dirt track and overtaking all others at the finish. What an introduction to horse racing!

Wendy is also a superb photographer with a eye for composition and the quickness to photograph horses racing down a track. Eventually we formed a business partnership which we worked on weekends. She was an elementary teacher, I worked at UCLA, so Saturdays and Sundays were the only available days. Our partnership was called BLS Photo, with the BLS standing for Black Leather Stables, looking ahead to when and if we ever owned a horse (which we never did, but she did under her own name after our business folded). Wendy was the photographer and I was the business person, although occasionally I'd take track pictures alongside her. We were authorized to photograph at the Southern California tracks and were called to Thoroughbred farms in California and Arizona to take pictures of horses, mostly "conformation" photos which were used for advertising purposes. We also sold her pictures as covers to Thoroughbred magazines and as models for artists. Finally, we would rent a booth at Thoroughbred auctions to simply sell the photos themselves as art.

We had the opportunity and pleasure of meeting some special people, being that the racing industry attracts celebrities: George Steinbrenner of New York Yankee fame, Robert Mitchum and his son, famous trainer Charlie Whittingham for whom we did work, jockey Bill Shoemaker who was featured in many of Wendy's photos as he won so many races, Mary Florsheim Jones of the Florsheim shoe fortune for whom we did a lot of work, actor James Brolin when we photographed on his ranch, actress Greer Garson who absolutely adored her horses and was always gracious to us, and many others.

The photography business was a wonderful interlude in our lives, but absolutely exhausting. Wendy got fairly well known as a Thoroughbred photographer, but we were working seven days a week. We continued the business for a while and eventually gave it up. We couldn't hold down full time jobs and be on call every weekend for photo jobs too. It was just too much work, despite how much fun it was at the same time.

But what came out of all this was a friendship that has lasted four decades, so far. Wendy recently took the picture of me on the cover, and forty years ago she took the front cover photo of me with my motorcycle. We've had our moments, of course, but all in all, we've been continuous friends most of that time. As I write this she has been with her partner, Marilee, for twenty-three years, and I feel as if Marilee has become a close friend also, if only by default. I know these two women would come to my rescue if I needed it, or leave me alone when I need that. They're both retired and I house sit for them when they're off on trips. I've taken vacations with Wendy when we were together, when we both were with partners, and in recent years when there was just the three of us. I have experienced traveling in a camper throughout the western states, National Parks, and camping which I never had done until Wendy came into my life. I have learned about the Thoroughbred Industry, which broadened my life experience enormously. But mostly, I discovered a friend for life.

39

My Major Intolerances

I haven't been writing about all the loves of my life, and certainly not about any of the one- or two-night stands. This isn't an *expose*, but an intent to put to paper memories of those people and events I believe were significant in my life. I write about those who helped to build my character and personality, so that anyone who is interested in knowing who I am, or what brought me to certain acts in the lesbian community, might have insight. By necessity that includes several women in my life. Most likely I would not have included this next person in my memoir, despite our being together for a couple of years, except that she brought out to me some of my intolerances, which was important to my personal growth.

When she was living with me, she had a drinking problem. This was not surprising as her grandmother, her mother, her mother's boyfriend, her father, and her father's second wife were all alcoholics. She could go without a drink for weeks, but she couldn't tolerate having just one drink. One drink would start her off on a binge, which usually led to violence, although never against me. I've known people who simply go quiet when they drink. I had one lover who had a cocktail every night before dinner to "help her relax." She only had one, and you'd never have realized she'd had even that. I've known others who go to sleep when they've had a bit too much to drink. It's amazing to me how people can act differently under the influence of the same drug–alcohol.

I didn't grow up with alcohol in my family at all, and therefore I had no personal knowledge of its effects until after I joined the Air Force. In the AF I got drunk a couple of times to the point of throwing up, decided I didn't like what it did to me and stopped drinking. We occasionally had a very tipsy woman in our lesbian bar in Germany, but we were in a closed society and her bed was very close by, so we took her to her room, put her to bed, and that was the end of that for the evening. What I did not experience was violence and lack of control as an adjunct to drinking. When this came into my life, it made me slow down and think about my reactions to these two subjects.

I'm not totally against drinking alcohol, even though I'm reluctant to kiss someone who has been drinking because I find the taste and smell of alcohol repugnant (as I do the smell of smoking, too), but I am against getting drunk. My research projects on drinking and driving at UCLA taught me that a very small amount of alcohol, one or two ounces, can significantly reduce a driver's reaction time, making driving a vehicle a very dangerous and life-threatening act. I also learned drunkenness resulting in violence can be risky. I would no longer live with someone who drinks more than a glass of wine or beer with dinner, or a beer on a hot summer afternoon.

As to violence, I do not comprehend that at all and have no place for it in my life. (For a more complete thought on violence against women see Section 6.) One time in my life I slapped a woman. It was not premeditated; it was reactive and quick. I'm sure the woman I slapped forgave me many, many years ago, even if she still remembers it. However, I have never forgotten nor forgiven myself, and will always be ashamed of that behavior.

40

Donna and Life Spring

When the relationship with my first U.S. lover, Virginia, ended after several years of trying to deal with her homophobia, I told myself I'd never get involved with a straight woman again. That resolve lasted about twenty years until I walked into a party with my co-workers and came face-to-face with Donna. She was my boss's ex-wife's sister (his ex-sister-in-law). I had been working at UCLA about fifteen years at that point, and couldn't believe I'd never come across her before. It turns out she came to the party with my boss because she had recently concluded divorcing her fourth husband and was bored.

Donna was a little taller than me, a bleached blond (as I was at the time), and convinced if she weighed anything over one hundred fifteen pounds she was "fat." She declared she was tired of everyone asking her if she realized she looked like Lauren Bacall, since they had been doing that for two decades. She was older than me by a few months, but between October and January we were the same age. She smoked, but when at home, she carried an ashtray around the house with her and when she finished her cigarette, she washed the ashtray and put it away. She was the one who had the one cocktail every day before dinner, but never showed the affects. And her home was always perfect; everything had its place and was never out of place. Did you say "anal retentive?" But, twenty years after my disasterous relationship with a straight woman, I was at it again, instant lust.

I was still living with another woman, but the relationship had ended with her unfaithfulness and my inability to cope with her drinking problem. The LN was a little more than a year old and growing. I was introduced to Donna and, after I picked my tongue up off the floor, fell all over myself paying attention to her the rest of the evening. She was invited (by others) to join our UCLA bowling league and that gave me the opportunity to get to know her better. Our relationship became hot rapidly, and I moved out of my apartment and into Donna's condo. I left practically everything behind–furniture, books, artwork–and paid the rent for my ex for three months.

As hot as this relationship was sexually in the beginning, it cooled for Donna just as rapidly. She had decades, and four husbands, to practice using sex as a tool to manipulate her partners, and she didn't hesitate to use it with me. Even though this relationship only lasted a couple of years, ending when she came in one night and told me to leave immediately, Donna changed my life drastically when she introduced me to Life Spring, a self awareness program which was an off-shoot from EST.

In January of 1978 Donna heard about Life Spring and decided to attend herself. The "Basic Training" or Level I Training was set up in a manner that allowed working people to attend Friday evening and the rest of the weekend. When Donna completed the program, she went on to take a Level II Training, which was longer and more intense. She was so determined that I would go to Life Spring, she offered to pay for my basic training course. Still hoping to make this relationship work, I agreed to go.

I cannot tell you details of the program itself as I swore an oath to not reveal the inner workings of Life Spring. Being the honest person I believe myself to be, I have not spoken of the behind-door training to anyone, not even the friends I have persuaded to take the training themselves. Life Spring has been described by others as a "kinder, gentler EST," meaning it has the same goals of assisting you in learning about yourself, but does so in a less harsh manner.

On the assumption you really do want to grow and learn about yourself, Life Spring engaged in exercises surrounding the discovery of who you are and what you believe. Their claim was that you would not learn anything you wouldn't have learned eventually anyway, but you'd get there much quicker. The exercises can be traumatic, depending on whether or not they apply to you. One tool used is sleep deprivation, another is discipline, but the trainers always seemed to be aware of each individual's reaction and well being.

There are those who go through the training and learn nothing, and there are those who change dramatically. I was one of the latter. The major change I experienced was that I was a very angry person, particularly angry at men when I started the program. By the end of the first level Life Spring training, that anger had melted away to...? Who knows? All I know is it was gone and hasn't returned in the more than a quarter of a century since Life Spring. I also went through the second level of training, which I paid for myself, and accepted many concepts of life I hadn't before, particularly the idea of personal accountability. Donna completed a third level of training in the middle of which she terminated our relationship.

There has been several times in my life since I accomplished my Life Spring training that it has "saved" me. I have been able to look upon whatever happened and accept that my life is exactly what I make of it and, however unpleasant it might seem at the moment, in the long run it is perfect and has led to the person I am today. One of those incidences of life was Donna's death, which I was able to embrace as a learning experience.

A few years after Donna and I broke up, she moved to Oregon. I went up to visit her for a week once a year, even though I was with someone else by then. When she was barely fifty-one it was discovered she had lung cancer, and within six months, despite surgery and radiation therapy, she had died. She told me she had started smoking when she was twelve. The last month of her life I went up to Oregon to be by her side until she passed, and then I stayed another month to inventory her house and assist her attorney in taking care of final business and her memorial. My mother had died quickly, as did my brother when he committed suicide, so I had no prior experience of lingering terminal illness. My Life Spring training lead me through that period and assisted me in soothing Donna's acceptance of her nearing death.

Donna has been gone more than twenty years now, and I doubt if a single day has gone by that I have not thought of her. Without question my life changed, *I* changed, because of a relatively short term partnership with a dynamic women who, I now believe, came into my life to expand my consciousness. If, as Life Spring teaches, there are no accidents, Donna was in my life to push me and teach me. When that was accomplished, she moved on physically, but shall always remain in my heart.

PART 5

THE LESBIAN NEWS STORY

41

The Saga of The Lesbian News Begins

The story of The Lesbian News really begins a couple of years prior to the first issue hitting the community. It begins at UCLA, moves to the Westside Women's Center, gets involved with the machinations at the Gay Community Service Center, and ends up the longest running lesbian newspaper in the world. This is a great example of how the inner-workings of the Los Angeles lesbian community adds to, or detracts from, all of us.

In the early 1970's three women decided to teach a class called The Lesbian Experience at the UCLA Experimental College. Just about anyone could teach anything at the evening Experimental College, so long as there was at least one person with a connection to UCLA heading the project. The coordinator had to be a student, professor, or employee on campus. One of the three was my lover at the time.

A prominent lesbian leader in our community was the connection to UCLA, and everything was in order. UCLA had approved the project, a room and time had been obtained, flyers had gone out and been posted, and people (mostly women) had signed up to attend the class. Then the UCLA connection pulled out of the project at the last minute. Because I was staff in the UCLA School of Engineering I was asked to fill in so The Lesbian Experience could continue.

I didn't have a clue as to what was expected of me, but quickly realized nothing was expected. The other two coordinators simply wanted my campus status to continue. Nevertheless I jumped in and participated as well as I could. By the end of the class I was ready to continue into the next school session. I learn quickly. Much to my surprise neither of the other coordinators were at all interested in continuing the class. They'd been there, done that, even though there were women asking if we were gong to give the class again. Thus it ended up that I taught The Lesbian Experience by myself for two more semesters, along with a wonderful collection of prominent lesbians from our community as guest speakers.

42

The Lesbian Activists Form

Out of the last Lesbian Experience class arose a group we called The Lesbian Activists. I use the word "Activists" here as the name of a specific group, not as a generalized term. There were, of course, many activists all over the nation beginning their own movements on various levels. Many of the women who had taken my class were strongly in favor of physically making themselves available for peaceful demonstrations like Take Back the Night marches, and other occasions where there was a need for a show of strength for our emerging lesbian/gay rights movement in the early to mid 1970s. This was a subject we had discussed in class and seem to strike a nerve in many women, some lesbian, some not.

Our intent was to create a telephone ladder where we could become available in a matter of hours, if not sooner. For example, Zee Budapest, a Wiccan leader who resided in Los Angeles at the time, used the reading of tarot cards as part of her religious practice. The City of Los Angeles decided such readings were not legitimate within the traditional religious community and insisted she obtain an "entertainment" license. She refused and was arrested. She asked members of The Lesbian Activists to monitor activities outside the courthouse when she was put on trial. We did, making sure any demonstrations were small and quiet, and monitoring the police presence as well. Zee and I had met when she was a speaker for The Lesbian Experience class on religion.

The Lesbian Activists also rallied for a demonstration at the West Los Angeles Federal Building, and we marched for the right to walk our streets at night without fear. Unfortunately the group turned out to be short lived. We met monthly at the Westside Women's Center located in Santa Monica. We would shoot the breeze, discuss what actions might use us, firm up and alter the telephone tree, and generally became a more closely knit group of about fifteen women.

It's important to know the Westside Women's Center was created and run by a group of radical lesbian/non-lesbian feminists who had the insight and courage to open such a center under adverse conditions and times. Remember, this was when you could be arrested for showing a woman how to use a speculum and mirror to examine herself. It was a time when police still walked through lesbian bars just to intimidate, without any real cause for entry, and there was nothing we could do about it.

In my opinion the women running the WWC were short-sighted for not realizing the diversity of our lesbian/women's community and the fact that all of us needed to work together was paramount to our success as a community. After all, it was the early beginnings, not long after the Christopher Street uprising. Unfortunately there still remains to this day some women in Los Angeles (and no doubt other communities), who have not yet reached the consciousness needed to realize cooperation gains more than divisiveness.

Meanwhile across town at the Gay Community Service Center, not yet to include lesbians in their title let alone other diversities, a brouhaha had arisen between management and some of the employees which resulted in the firing of several lesbians and gay men from the Center. The accounting of their problems must be left to those who were directly involved and who know much more than I about the details.

However, the result of the firings was far reaching in the community. The women running the WWC polled the various groups meeting at "their" center, which had taken the side of the fired employees and was demanding action against GCSC. Very simply, if your group did not support the fired employees, you were no longer welcome at the WWC. The Lesbian Activists discussed their position and decided, from what we knew, there was wrong-doing on both sides of the issue. Therefore they voted to remain neutral. Not acceptable! We were asked to leave the Center.

There was one small monthly newspaper in Los Angeles at the time, *Sister* newspaper, run by some of the same women who were associated with the WWC. The Lesbian Activists sought to have their group meeting time and place included in the paper's monthly calendar. Same women, same result: we were not welcome! The only other publication out of Los Angeles, *The Lesbian Tide*, was more of a political magazine, and did not afford any kind of space for our recognition.

This exclusion due to disagreement pissed the hell out of me, and I said to a few of my Activist friends, "If we can't be in their publications, we'll start our own!" This was the demise of The Lesbian Activists, and the beginning of *The Lesbian News*.

43

The Lesbian News is Born

The Lesbian News was born in August 1975. It was two sheets of 8 1/2x11" paper (four pages) stapled in the upper left hand corner. It was an inauspicious beginning. We stuck it under windshields of cars in lesbian bar parking lots with a headline that screamed: WHO ARE WE? It was placed on cigarette machines in lesbian bars, and promptly thrown out by some management as soon as we left the building. We printed 500 copies of Issue 1, paid for out of my own pocket, and I'm sure 450 or more were tossed without ever being read.

The next month we came back with a four sheet/eight page issue and a logo contest. I suspect more copies were ignored than read, but we persevered and gradually began to realize we were being acknowledged by some women. Within two years *Sister Newspaper* was gone and we were printing a couple of thousand copies of the LN each month. More importantly, we had enough advertising to pay the printing costs. We published totally with volunteers.

We had lots to say about the need in our community for a publication that was open to all members and, during my leadership, we opened the LN pages to every lesbian/women's group, even ones I didn't personally support. Admittedly, I balked at the inclusion of the Gay Nazis. I could not bring myself to accept such a concept or be part of it. As it didn't appear to include lesbians, I had an excuse to exclude them from the LN. To the best of my memory, that was the only time I refused to accept submissions from a group, although there were a few times when accepting material caused me a big headache or a loss of advertising revenue.

When we made the request for advertising, the first women to respond were therapists. Early on we had several therapists for each non-therapist ad. One evening at a party I was taken to task about the ads in the LN. I was accused of making it look like the lesbian community in Los Angeles was all crazy since most of the ads featured local therapists offering their services. After staring blankly for a moment or two, I shrugged my shoulders and suggested these women put their money where their mouth was and supported what we were doing, and if other women and businesses wanted to join us, they would be welcome, too. By the time the LN was self supporting financially, therapist ads were mixed in between many others and not so noticeable. However, I will always be appreciative of the many therapists in our community who supported us from the beginning and by doing so, made others take notice. Thirty years later, there are a few of the original supporters still advertising in the LN!

I started out writing and editing everything myself. Soon we asked a few women to contribute columns. We added book reviews, more advertising, community calendars, an events column, and more news. Mostly news. We exchanged publications with groups from all over the U.S. and reprinted items we thought were newsworthy and appropriate to our community. We added a few exchanges with foreign publications written in English, and added international news. We included everything we were asked to print, including classified ads for jobs and housing, but not personals.

Personal ads were a bug-a-boo with me. I was convinced if we allowed them, they would degenerate to being sexist, lookist, ageist, racist, and any other ist you can think of. Eventually we did begin taking personals, but kept a very strict eye on the editing. Basically you could describe yourself, but you couldn't specify what you were looking for as to physical attributes. After all, you could make decisions about whether or not the person fit your desires when you spoke or wrote to her. I still like our concept of personal ads better than the current ones.

I got hell from the community when we took our first 800 sex line ads. Our position was that they were part of the community and the reader of the LN had a choice to call the number or not. However, because of the consequences of alcoholism, and the incidences of alcoholism in the lesbian community, we did not solicit advertising for alcoholic beverages, and no company ever offered.

Which brings up the question, who is "we?" I was publisher and editor of *The Lesbian News* for its first fourteen years. During my ownership, the LN was entirely produced and distributed by volunteers, sometimes as many as 40 or more on staff at the same time. No one was paid a salary, although at one period delivery women were reimbursed for gasoline and columnists were paid five dollars per column to cover the costs of paper and postage. When there was a short fall in advertising revenue, the LN was financially supported out of my personal pocket, which wasn't all that deep. In order to succeed we needed to accomplish each issue with as little money as possible since the LN was distributed free of charge.

We did not attempt to sell the LN because our philosophy was to get as many lesbians to read it as possible. Many of the papers were put into bars, and most women, if faced with limited income, would rather have another beer than read a newspaper. That's not a condemnation, it's a fact. If I were in their situation, I might make the same choice. Besides, collecting the money from the bars would have been a nightmare! Although they allowed us to put the newspapers in the bar, they really didn't want anything to do with them, particularly in the beginning. Being free was the best way to get women to actually read the LN. That was the important bottom line to us.

I've been asked how I could handle all those volunteers. It appears other organizations have not been as successful as I was. Remember, we had to meet a monthly deadline and when we were up to 32 pages or more, we had many people working on each issue. I believe there are four reasons it worked:

...I never asked any one women to do too much. If it was a big job, I asked as many women as necessary to assist. For example, several women helped type, but no one typed more than two or three hours a month.

...I understood being a volunteer lasts only so long. When a woman wanted to leave, I sincerely thanked her for her time and wished her well.

...When someone failed to do her job, I let her go. I sincerely thanked her for her previous contributions and suggested it just wasn't the right time in her life to continue with us. In short, I fired a non-producing volunteer, as gently as I could. I've been told you can't fire a volunteer. I've never taken that position.

...When there was a hole in the work load, I filled it myself. There were many holes: editing, typing, paste-up, delivery, bookkeeping, and others. I did a lot of the work myself!

Personal relationships were difficult over the last reason. The women I was with (three in fourteen years) never seemed to understand my committment to the LN and that meeting a deadline was important. They told me the closer it was to deadline, the more intense I became and the more time I spent on the LN, leaving less time for them. And this happened monthly. In retrospect, I would admit to spending half of my time away from my regular job on the LN, and half on my relationship. However, in the years I published the LN, I was late on the streets (meaning after the first of the month) only three times. Once a person from Sisterhood Bookstore called asking where the LN was a week before it was due! When I replied it wasn't the first of the month yet, I was told they thought it was late because it was usually early! How's that for logic?

Every woman who volunteered to work on the LN, in what ever way, was a "staff" member. After a few years of heading up the LN by myself, I had the bright idea I would create a Board of Directors to assist in making decisions about the publication. Any staff member could run for the Board, and were voted on by secret ballot of all staff member's who were present at the meeting. In general those who volunteered were close to my own philosophy about the LN, and there was little conflict. Women who totally disagreed with me didn't volunteer their time. There were a couple of instances, however, I didn't care for the decision. One of those was about taking personal ads. Since I created the Board, it was only right I follow their recommendations, and I did. One friend told me as head of the LN I was a "benevolent dictator" until the Board came along. You know what? I like the title "benevolent dictator." Unfortunately I've never had that opportunity again.

After the tenth anniversary of the LN I realized it was time to think about either shutting down the publication or finding the right someone to take over. I was proud of what the LN had done for our community. I knew it was needed as no other paper had appeared. And the community itself had told me of its importance through awards and recognitions. I realized I just couldn't shut it down, but it was time for me to let go. In our community it's call "burn out."

It took nearly three and a half years to find a women I thought would do justice to the LN, Deborah, although we didn't start out on a good note. I had been approached by several people with inquiries, but most women didn't have any real idea about the commitment that would be necessary. Or they didn't want to pay the price. Yes, I sold the LN; I did not give it away. After all those years of work without pay, it would seem okay to want some actual money from the LN, but that wasn't the reason.

When I began to seriously contemplate letting go of the paper, I realized a significant amount of money paid by the new owner would be the only way the LN would have a chance to survive. If I gave it away, and whoever I gave it to discovered it was a lot more work than they had wanted, it would be easy to just shut it down. After all, they had not invested anything in keeping the LN publishing.

But I had invested nearly fourteen years of my life in the LN, and wanted it to at least have a chance to continue. I had established a small subscription list of those who paid for receiving the LN through the mail and I had accumulated a continuous advertiser list, which was enough to pay for the LN's publication each month. Finally, and most importantly, I had created a great reputation and a place in the community for the paper. The latter may not be a tangible asset, but was its greatest value.

When I first spoke to Deborah, she seemed sincere to me. She was a reporter for the Los Angeles Times, so already knew about meeting deadlines and some aspects of publishing. I told her I was asking twenty thousand dollars for the LN, and she didn't seem phased by the amount. A few days later I received a contract in the mail from her, with a caveat it needed to be signed within three days or it was cancelled. I immediately called her and told her to forget it, I did not respond well to being pressured, and she could consider the contract cancelled. I also told her I didn't consider the tone of the contract as being feminist. Deborah did a double take, admitted the contract had been prepared by a male attorney, and asked if we could start over. I agreed to that, without any attorneys. Eventually we came to an agreement and she purchased the LN from me.

She didn't skip an issue and needed some assistance at the very beginning, so I volunteered back to her to help with typing. I know she was very leary of my being around when she took over. I suspect she thought I would try and tell her how to do things. But that's not my style. When I turned the LN over to Deborah, it was no longer mine, and I never made a suggestion to her. Had I not been ready to give up the LN, I'd have not done so. Having done so, I would not show lack of respect for Deborah by interfering. I came to her apartment, I typed, I left. I volunteered only for a few months and went on my way, never looking back. I never regretted my decision to let go; my time with the LN had run its course.

44

A Note About Being Paid

In 2005 I was interviewed by historian Lillian Faderman in regard to *The Lesbian News* for a history of the gay and lesbian movement in Los Angeles. In her research she read many of the early issues of the LN, and brought up the fact in our interview that I had written about the importance of women being fairly paid for their work, yet neither I nor the staff were paid for our time on the LN.

I only had to think about that for a moment to realize that the LN wasn't work, it was an avocation. Everyone who shared her time working on the LN did so because she realized this was an important project in the lesbian community.

No one ever mentioned pay to me and I don't believe anyone thought of it. Yes, I sold the LN and took the money at the end, but not as delayed pay. That would have worked out to about ten cents an hour or less! As I mentioned, I sold the LN because that was the only way to have a good chance the newspaper would survive, which it has.

I still believe women should be paid fairly for their work. I've worked for one level of government or another most of my life. Although I've experienced equal pay for equal work, as well as the reversal of that when I worked in the electronic industry, I realize most women have not. This fight is not yet over.

45

Looking Back, Looking Forward

The question I'm most asked years after I turned The Lesbian News over to Deborah and it has gone through another sale to Ella, is how do I feel about the changes in the LN.

Changes? Nobody made more changes than I did! The physical look progressed from stapled sheets of 8 1/2x11 bond, to 11x17 folded bond, to folded newsprint, to tabloid size as it is now. We added one color, then two, for accents. When I finally gave up publishing the LN after fourteen years, we were close to going to a full color cover, which Deborah did. The number of pages we printed increased year after year until our average was 64 tabloid size pages per month. For anniversary issues, we printed from 72 to as much as 104 pages. But these are only physical attributes and not as important as the content.

I started out editing or writing every thing myself. We added columnists. We added book reviews, movie reviews, more advertising, community calendars, splitting the LN into specific area sections (Los Angeles, Orange County, San Diego, etc). We added event columns and more national and international news, although we kept our focus on Southern California. We took the first 800 sex line ads and classified advertising. We added photographs and color accents. And that's only the beginning of the changes we made.

We needed forty percent advertising space to break even. I haven't actually counted the advertising space allotment in the LN in the Twenty-First Century, but I would guess it to be at least sixty percent. Much more of it is full page ads, and the price to advertise in the LN is several times higher than what I needed to charge. Part of that is because the staff is now paid, which is a good thing; part of the need for more revenue is the fact that it's published with full color, which is quite expensive, and of course paper and printing costs have sky-rocketed.

Change is inevitable. If our community changes, the LN will change with it. I rarely see ads any more of butch looking lesbians in the LN. Both the ads and the photos picture "lipstick lesbians." I don't see myself or my friends in the paper. But that's because the community is now made up of a larger percent of younger lesbians who don't necessarily believe in the butch/femme roles or find the need to wear boots and flannel shirts with their Levis. They're more into designer jeans and blouses, and if they are wearing boots, they're high-heeled.

Is this change in either the community or the LN wrong? Of course not! It's just what is, and the LN reflects the community. My generation is dying off. Most of the lesbians in Los Angeles have never even heard my name and don't associate me with the LN. Who looks at the small type at the bottom of a staff list? I actually called the LN office one day to asked about possible advertising, and the women who worked there didn't know my name. I know because I asked. And Ella does not acknowledge my existence; I'm not even invited to the LN's anniversary parties, despite my being the founder.

I'm glad the police no longer walk through the lesbian bars just to intimidate us. I'm glad teenage boys let us walk the sidewalks without yelling at us from their passing cars. I'm glad we can fight legislation and win, and lobby for rights no one ever thought about before Christopher Street. I'm particularly glad my friend Wendy was named Teacher of the Year in the Pasadena School District with the full knowledge she was an open lesbian.

These and many other changes are positive and, hopefully, more positive changes are on the horizon. Younger lesbians simply don't realize they have the freedom to be themselves today because we stood up to be counted years before they were born. And that's as it should be.

The Lesbian News was born out of controversy. Early on we knew it would either fade away when the controversy ended, or become something special. I believe I gave it a good foundation and Deborah nurtured it and brought it technically into a new age. Ella has done what I could not do, pay the people who bring the LN to the community each month. As I write this, the LN has passed its thirtieth birthday and I hope that Ella, or maybe a new dedicated owner, will support the continuance of the LN which has become the longest running lesbian newspaper in the world. Yes, the LN is special, even if I am biased. The entire community should be as proud of their support over these many years as I am of founding it in the first place.

In 2006 I was named a "Feminist Who Changed America" in a book with the same name by Barbara Love. I was chosen for my founding The Lesbian News. Despite the local awards I received for the newspaper, the national recognition came as a surprise. I know the LN would not have succeeded originally without my personal dedication–along with the many volunteers–and I'm pleased with the acknowledgment of my hard work which gave the LN its base to continue for so many years. May it live forever, or at least for as long as our community needs it.

PART 6

ACTIVISM & OBSERVATIONS

46

A Brief Introduction To This Section

I have reached a place in my autobiography where some of my memories are more general. Please keep in mind I lived through this awakening of lesbian rights and sensibilities, and sometimes remember and see things in a more general way than specific events. I want to write about the *gestalt* of the time as well as the specifics, and will do so in this section.

Remember also that these writings are my own interpretation of the era, and had significant influence on who I have become in my older life. Others, with different backgrounds, would react to this time period differently. Whereas it was easy to pick out events that changed my life in my younger days, even minutely at the time, as I have gotten older my life events are more broadly based. Our learning curve is said to be the steepest on the day we are born, thus it makes sense that as we embrace life experiences, it makes less of an impact on the "who" that we are.

Let this introduction serve as acceptance of these writings as my insight. I own all that I say, and do not expect the reader to agree with me. If it reads as if I am making some general assumption about everyone lumped together, please forgive my ineptitude to make myself clear. At all times I am writing from my personal perspective, and not for the community in general.

47

N.O.W. & The Lesbian Rights Task Force

Before The Lesbian Experience classes I taught at UCLA, you could safely say I was pretty non-political. And remember, I "fell" into teaching those classes. I really had no conscious intention of being either a feminist or an activist.

Prior to all this "stuff" beginning to change my life, I spent my non-working time bowling two or three leagues a week, occasionally going out to the bars (although eventually I no longer drank alcohol), and making out with just about any woman who would have me. When I was young I had this desire to make love to ninety percent of the women on the earth. That percentage dropped as I got older and realized so many women weren't worth fucking, even for one night. Alternatively, when there was no woman in my life, I'd become despondent.

My working time, nearly twenty years in traffic safety research, entailed very long, productive and rewarding days. Without a doubt this was the best job of my life. It was exciting, rewarding intellectually and financially, boosted my self esteem, led to the emergence of the LN, and allowed me to participate in an occupation that did good for humanity. Who could ask for more?

But when the Lesbian Experience classes came along, and from that the Lesbian Activists and subsequently *The Lesbian News*, my life began to change. Have you notice here the reoccurance of the word lesbian? I was determined to be "out there" with my lesbianism and ready to label everything with that title. I had never been deeply closeted, even in the military, and totally out since I was twenty-two, more than fifty years ago. By necessity a string of events, which included the firings at the Gay Community Service Center, engaged me in political activism I could never have imagined before then.

However, as are all events in one's life, it was exactly the right time. Stonewall had happened and hundreds of thousands of gay men and lesbians decided they were going to stop hiding, even if still afraid, and damn the consequences! I can't remember ever being afraid in regards to my being a lesbian, but I was cautious. I'd lost one job because I was a lesbian, and at the same time I was willing to attend lesbian bars despite the emotional abuse practiced there by the heterosexual hierarchy. Early on the bars were owned by straight males. Although men don't like us, they've never hesitated to make money off of us.

When I started publishing *The Lesbian News* I also became aware of other political activities in our community. One of those was the National Organization for Women and its Lesbian Rights Task Force. The main focus for NOW at that time was the passage of the Equal Rights Amendment, without a doubt their greatest failure.

My basic interest when I joined NOW was the Lesbian Rights Task Force (LRTF), which (at that time) held a semi-autonomous position in the Los Angeles Chapter of NOW. Although the Task Force was formed under auspices of LA NOW, and sought approval from the Chapter Board of Directors for their projects, they pretty much planned and executed those activities on their own. In fact, there were times when we complained about lack of interest and support from our home chapter.

The LRTF even had its own checking account separate from the Chapter's and controlled solely by the Task Force. This was a really big sore spot for LA NOW, the members of which wanted all money associated with the Chapter under their control, mainly to be used for the fight for the ERA. The Task Force, while supporting and working for the ERA along with Chapter sisters, had other, lesbian, interests they pursued. I was on the Task for about four years and we did some good work during that time as well as supporting the ERA.

Our main yearly project was a two-day Lesbian Conference held on the USC campus. We spent the better part of the year preparing for two days that produced most of the income for the year for the Task Force. We had a USC employee contact who arranged for our use of the campus and its class rooms without charge. We offered workshops on just about any women or lesbian topic you could think of and asked the best experts in our community to lead them.

The conference attracted hundreds of women and lesbians and was highly successful. The biggest complaint we had was that we offered so many different workshops to choose from in any time slot attendees had difficulty in deciding which ones to attend! Many workshops filled quickly and nearly all were well attended. Pre-registration was primarily by mail and workshops were filled on a first come, first served basis. We had a Saturday lunch time speaker of repute and offered box lunches to those who had pre-ordered with their registration. I have never before or after attended a lesbian conference in the Southern California area that was so well organized and displayed so much enthusiasm and joy by its attendees. I had the honor of co-chairing the last one held before the Task Force disintegrated.

The problem was the money. The LA Chapter had gotten progressively demanding that the Task Force give up its own bank account and simply turn the proceeds over to them. No matter the money was above board and put to good use, the Chapter wanted control. For the years I was with them, the Task Force had made its own decisions about where the money was spent. First we held out seed money for the next year's conference (flyers, ads, registration forms, postage, copying, etc.). Secondly, at least fifty percent went directly to the Chapter for its general fund, which we thought was appropriate.

The remaining money was designated to be returned to the lesbian community. We solicited requests for grants from organizations and individuals in Los Angeles, and funded the ones the Task Force felt reasonable and worthy. The smaller the monetary request and the more appropriate it was to the lesbian community, the more likely it was funded. We felt good about returning profits to the community that supported us and the conference.

After the conference I co-chaired, the Board demanded the Task Force bank account be closed or they threatened to disband the Task Force altogether. They had that right. During the last year of my association with LA NOW and the LRTF, I also served as the Task Force liaison to the Board, so I was able to observe the situation from both sides. What I experienced was purely a power play on the Board's side, apparently wanting to spend all money available on the ERA, which was losing. The Task Force members thought they had been doing a good job, including raising a goodly sum for the ERA project, and simply wanted the *status quo* to continue. The result was not good.

The bank account was closed and the seed money for the next conference transferred to the Chapter. Frankly, none of us on the Task Force thought there was a chance in hell of LA NOW funding the next year's lesbian conference. As a protest all the hardworking leadership resigned from the Task Force and from NOW. The handful of remaining members of the LRTF who remained had little experience. For all practical purposes the Task Force was gutted and ceased to effectively exist. Sadly, there were no more conferences that I'm aware of and The Equal Rights Amendment failed to pass.

I understand the Lesbian Rights Task Force of LA NOW was reinstituted, but I've never heard about any great work being done by them since we resigned *en mass*. Frankly, since the failure of the ERA, I haven't experienced NOW having much success either.

It appears to me that the LA NOW vs LRTF situation was a classic example of turning a win-win relationship into a lose-lose one. The year I spent on the chapter Board was eye-opening and very disappointing. I had hoped women who had been oppressed all their lives would have learned to do things in a different, better way. After listening to the bickering, experiencing the behind scenes power struggles, and being personally oppressed by mostly straight women I was led to believe were my "sisters," I realized they only knew how to function as their patriarchal examples had taught them. How depressing!

48

Take Back the Night and Other Fallacies

I'm writing this memoir in the Twenty-First Century, and you cannot tell that back in the 1970's we took action to reclaim our right to walk down a street at night, alone. We couldn't do that forty years ago, and we still can't do it today. In fact, it may be less likely now to be able to walk alone at night without being molested in some way–robbed, beaten, raped.

I once edited a lesbian writer of short stories whose fiction always had happy, Pollyanna-like endings. I questioned her about this simply out of curiosity. She told me she wrote stories as she believed life *should* be, not necessarily as it was. Was she naive? I don't think so; I think she recognized her endings were wishful thinking, and happy endings were "her thing." On the other hand I believe the lesbian community *was* naive back when we thought we had the power to change things by simply bringing a problem to the forefront by such actions as marching in the streets. We got attention, for about a minute and a half, and were soon forgotten. The good news is that when we were in force in the streets we were safe, at least for that night.

The bad news is that actual change is slow to take place and it happens only when action is continuous. A handful of night marches didn't change a thing and was quickly forgotten. The very simple Equal Rights Amendment guaranteeing women equal rights with men has never been reintroduced in Congress since its defeat. Whereas when a few women decided it was time women should be able to vote and sit on juries, (did you know juries were male-only throughout history, even when judging a female defendant, until after women obtained the vote?), they didn't stop protesting and being jailed until they succeeded in their quest.

After the protests, marches, defeat of the Briggs Initiative in California (to disallow any lesbian or gay person from teaching in public schools, no matter if they were actively gay or lesbian, or were heterosexuals advocating alternative life-styles), publicity, rise of lesbian/gay centers and pride parades, masses of individual's jumping out of their closets at work and home, and the passage of a few non-discrimination clauses in major cities and prominent companies and institutions during the late 1980s and through the '90s, the community ceased to be a community at all. Lesbian centers and bookstores closed. Publicity was non-existent, unless you count a lesbian serial murderer or a gay man who ate parts of his young, male victims. It is *not* true that any publicity is good publicity.

The good public guys and gals didn't start coming out of their personal closets until the turn of the Twenty-First Century. I believe this ten year gap of non-activism on a large scale (the increase in lesbian bars doesn't count), is the reason the religious far right has become so strong in politics. They don't give up after a defeat; they work harder. They get out the vote, electing candidates who support their agenda, including anti-gay/lesbian legislation. The gains we have achieved, like Domestic Partnership, can be rescinded.

Now, in the new century, lesbians and gays have come to life again. Having gained some relationship protection and responsibilities under Domestic Partnership laws, they want to leapfrog over Civil Unions and go directly to marriage. Good idea under the concept of equal rights in the U.S. which, although stated in our Constitution, is not and never was practiced in reality. Maybe we ask too much, too quickly? In June 2008 The California Supreme Court struck down an initiative passed in California limited marriage to a man and a woman. Quickly opponents qualified an amendment to the State Constitution for the November 2008 ballot which would outlaw gay marriage. This book will go to press before the results of that vote is known. Meanwhile thousands of lesbians and gays have taken the opportunity to marry in California.

I'm separated by two generations from the young people of today. On one side that makes me an old fogey. On the other, it gives me a perspective of history the impatient youngsters cannot appreciate. They think of my generation as being too cautious. They don't understand that at the time we were active, *we* were equally impatient, and so charged by older members of our community who were afraid to come out of their personal closet. We old activists, who are now beginning to die off, started from a place of hiding our sexual orientation, being fired from our jobs if found out to be gay/lesbian, being thrown out of our families and for some, never being spoken to again by our parents, and generally being oppressed because of who we were. Thanks to the work by Parents and Friends of Gays, Gay Pride

Parades, out-of-the-closet attitudes, and a few lesbian/gay and gay-accepting legislators, most young people don't have to start at the level we older people did. Most, at least in metropolitan areas where lesbians congregate, are free to be themselves. If not a perfect life, at least we opened some doors young lesbians today don't have to break down to pass through.

What I fear is this persistent push toward legal marriage between same sex couples gives the far right constituents something to point to that even fairminded supporters can say, "Now that's going too far!" I fear a backlash which will push even reasonable people to vote for the amendment. If I had been aboard that bandwagon, I would have pushed for equal rights with heterosexuals under Civil Unions. I would have pushed for more after Civil Unions had been around a number of years and absorbed into society. Demanding "marriage" now, which carries no more legal rights than a civil union, may backfire. Only time will tell.

What amazes me, however, is the concept of lesbians working to act like heterosexuals. Straight couples statistically end up in divorce fifty percent of the time. Lesbian couples end up in two or more relationships eighty to ninety percent of the time. There are those who say the high rate of coupling and uncoupling is because there are no legal obligations to separating, and thus no reason to try to stay together. If lesbians could legally marry, does that mean we could end up separating only fifty percent of the time? I guess that would be an improvement, but it would also entail a lot more time and cost, and lawyers would make a financial killing. At least, hopefully, they would be lesbian divorce attorneys and the money would stay in the community.

Now if we could only get lesbian owned/operated grocery stores, clothing boutiques, shoe stores, gas stations, etc., we could be a real community. We already have plenty therapists, hairdressers, and aforementioned lawyers. We also have a handful of doctors, dog trainers, and financial advisors. Personally, I can't find any of those close to me in the San Fernando Valley. However, my general physician, dentist, dermatologist, podiatrist, optometrist, chiropractor, lawyer, and insurance agent are all women. One of them is black, one Russian, one Chinese, one Iranian, one Jewish and three white. I used to have a lesbian mechanic, but she disappeared out of my life. The mechanic I now have has a lesbian daughter and is understanding. That gives him more status with me than most males. My hairdresser is a male, but he's gay and has been a friend for more than twenty-five years.

Maybe they're not all lesbians, but at least most of them are women, and all of them are supportive, knowing I'm a lesbian. I try to put my money where my mouth is. If all lesbians did that, we could really show some monetary clout, which translates to power. Oh well, I can only dream like my Pollyanna writer.

49

Male Privilege

I mentioned earlier in this memoir that I never experienced penis envy, but was always upset over male privilege. It is a very real situation in our society, and in most cultures of the world, that women suffer from the institution of male privilege, resulting not only in economical deficiency, but low self esteem, less education, and a reduced desire to succeed.

It is my belief that the male physique of larger size, body weight and more muscle in the human species could be overcome if males were not given privileges and psychological bolstering from birth, mostly by their mothers. Thus women perpetuate their own suppression by how they raise their male children.

Conversely, female children are raised with lower and different expectations, even in this Twenty-first Century. Fathers can amplify the dichotomy in how their children are raised if they're in the family unit. If they participate in rearing their children at all, it usually (but not always) widens the discrepancy between how male and female children learn their place in our society. Now we have *both* parents reinforcing male privilege. And it all pisses the hell out of me because I know without question I'm more intelligent, efficient, competent and caring than ninety percent of men.

Male privilege applies to gay men as well, as they were brought up by the same mothers in the same society with the same expectations as straight men. Although sexual orientation may be set at a very early age, as I believe it was for me, none of us actually comprehend this as young children. Therefore our early socialization is the same as those individuals who do not turn out to be gay or lesbian. Despite this equal start in life, perpetrated most of the time by straight parents, somewhere along the line we separate ourselves from non-gays to express our desired sexuality.

Now lesbians are consciously becoming mothers and raising children. Studies have shown that about the same percentage of children from gay parents become gay or lesbian themselves as do from straight parents. But I would hope that lesbian mothers are treating their male and female children more equally and are the leading edge of equalizing expectations between men and women. There are also enlightened straight women who understand the problem of male privilege and are attempting to teach their young children a more equal position in life. The question is whether it's too late to make a difference.

Like a snowball running down hill, male privilege has picked up speed during my lifetime, and does not appear to be reversing itself. Throughout history women and children have been beaten, raped and killed by men who believe they have the *right* to those actions with little, if any, punishment. In the United States we have enacted more and stronger laws against domestic assault, rape, and murder but without any cessation of those crimes. It is my belief the hubris necessary to commit these acts against others, and to frequently get away with them, is due to male privilege.

50

S&M and Violence Against Women

The Take Back the Night demonstrations were aimed at heterosexual men in the most part. However our lesbian community doesn't have to go outside itself to find violence against women. I suspect the percentages are very similar between heterosexual and lesbian couples, but I have no desire to prove this one way or the other. The fact has already been proven scientifically that most children who are raised in an abusive home, grow up to be abusive adults. There is no logic in believing being a lesbian changes this learned behavior. The inclusion of alcohol and/or other drugs doesn't help the problem.

In the lesbian community physical abuse of one's partner is mostly kept private and hidden, except when it comes to sadomasochistic activities, which are frequently displayed proudly. S&M advocates claim this kind of violence against women is all right because it is "consensual." Even if you apply that concept to S&M, it is my belief that violence is still violence.

If a man slaps his wife around and she lets him do this because she has no place else to go, thinks she/he still love each other, wants to keep the family together for the sake of the children, etc, she is consenting to his abuse as a condition of their relationship. If a lesbian slaps her wife around for the same reasons, only she verbalizes the consent, it's declared all right. Not in my opinion.

My objection in our community is not with S&M *per se*, but with the idea some women have that they can redefine common usage of words to fit whatever scenario they want to present, and once they change the meaning, it cleans up the image. If a sadist likes to hurt women, fine. If a masochist likes to be hurt, physically or emotionally, fine. It's their right to be who they wish to be. All I ask is the acts be called what they really are: assault, abuse, violence.

Where did we learn this behavior? From the heterosexual families from which the majority of us came forth. It saddens me that many lesbians perpetrate and imitate all the bad heterosexual behaviors learned at society's knee, as well as the good ones. I want us to be mature enough to tell the difference, reject negative behavior, and embrace positive ones.

I bring up this topic because I spent two years in a relationship with a woman who became, apparently, proud of her standing in the S&M community. The time we spent together profoundly influenced me. When we were together she was not into S&M, and never physically abused me. When she began to emotionally abuse me, I terminated the relationship. No way would I share my life with some one who did not respect me.

If you believe, as I do, that everything is a learning experience, whether or not you actually learn the lesson, then I see this period as a time in my life as the opportunity within which I solidified my personal beliefs on violence against women, or anyone else.

When I was a teenager I visited my brother Bill on the "ranch" he managed in the Napa area. Besides growing wine grapes, they had orchards of walnuts, as well as apple and other fruit trees. They also had a lot of squirrels, which were considered pests as they ate the nuts and fruit. Not being as smart at that age as I eventually became, I took my brother's .22 calibre rifle out one day to shoot those pesky squirrels. Into the trees I tramped looking for a target, and there was one, sitting on a branch and looking down at me no more than ten feet away. I raised the rifle, took deadly aim, pulled the trigger, and missed! Even a small bore rifle makes a bit of noise, and normally I would expect the squirrel to run away, but it didn't. The squirrel sat on the branch literally gazing into my eyes. I took aim a second time, shot the rifle, and the squirrel fell to the ground, dead.

I had thought nothing beforehand about going out to kill squirrels, but as I stood there looking at the dead squirrel at my feet, I realized I had just killed a living, breathing, animal and I was devastated! Yes, I'd killed spiders, stepped on ants and bugs before. But somehow this was different. I viewed the squirrel as a peaceful being who had just been doing his natural thing in life eating nuts and fruits and really hurting no one. I took the rifle back to the ranch house and put it away, but I have never forgotten that squirrel gazing down on me before I took its life.

I believe there is only one reason for violence of any kind, and that's for self-defense, whether personally or nationally. You may consider this stance strange coming from someone who spent sixteen years in the military. Two factors mitigate that in my mind. First, I hadn't formulated this position at eighteen years old when I joined up to get away from home. And second, I quit the Air Force with less than four years to go to qualify for a pension because I could no longer support the military. This was during the Viet Nam War. I withdrew from the AF consciously knowing I would forfeit all benefits. I had come to realize taking a personal stance against war and violence was more important than personal benefits. I have not regretted my decision for one moment.

If it comes to self-defense, however, violence becomes a different issue. If my country was invaded again, as it was at the beginning of WWII by Japan (and I was eight years old and impressionable), I would defend it. If my home was invaded by a thief and I was personally threatened, I would "shoot first and ask questions later." Odds are such invaders would be male, for whom I have little respect anyway. Even if they were women, and even if I am against violence, I would not lie down and be trampled by others. I have too much self-respect.

I am against violence, but I'm not a pacifist. There is a difference.

51

Mort Sahl's Call for Genocide

(Note: In this section I use last names. I do so only because the action I report below was well documented in the media, both print and electronic, and the names are a matter of public record.)

In the 1980's Mort Sahl, who *TV Guide* calls a "satirist," was host of his own television show in Los Angeles shown on local Channel 13, call letters KCOP (if I remember correctly). That station is now owned by a different company. In general I support individual rights to personal opinions and his or her right to express them no matter how bigoted. But there are limitations.

For example, "freedom of speech" does *not* include a right to shout "fire" in a theater or other crowded, public location, where such action could cause bodily harm to others in an attempt to exit a seemingly dangerous situation which was falsely activated. Freedom of speech is not an acceptable claim when defaming a person, or when inciting a riot which also might lead to bodily harm.

But one night on his program, highly homophobic Mort Sahl did in fact call for the annihilation of all lesbians and gays. He did this on public airways! The gay community was already plagued with being beaten up by police, teenagers, skinheads and anyone else who thought themselves above the law. Sahl was now attempting to legitimize such action and spur on the perpetrators to lesbian/gay genocide. The community reacted immediately.

I was not party to the initial contact between Channel 13 and the community, and cannot speak to the process, but the result was the station and Sahl agreed to air a program featuring two lesbian/gay representatives. Those two were long-time community activist Morris Kight, and Christopher Street West Committee President Sharon Cornelison.

When the appointed night arrived, studio seats were full of members of our community, and I and my friends were there to support our two representatives. Besides Sahl, Morris and Sharon, Geoff Edwards, a radio disc jockey, was present as a third guest or a co-host. I never quite understood why he was there at all considering the sensitivity of the subject to be discussed.

The program started out smoothly enough, but it was apparent from the beginning that there was never going to be agreement between the gay community and Sahl. As the interviews and opinions progressed, exchanges between Morris, Sharon and Sahl became heated. Soon after, Edwards stood up, lifted his hands in the air and said something to the effect of "I don't need this" and walked off the set. Not too long after, a vitriolic Mort Sahl also left the set, indicating he wouldn't go on with the program which was being taped.

It was obvious to the audience at this point that the community wasn't going to get the air time they had been promised, but nobody left the studio. After milling around a bit, Morris and others conferred and the consensus was we'd simply stay and occupy the studio until something else could be worked out with the station. KCOP management personnel came in to warn us that we were responsible for the expensive television equipment, which they had covered up. Morris assured them we were not interested in destruction, and was planning a peaceful sit-in. Ultimately, when we left three days later, the equipment was unharmed.

Members of the lesbian/gay leadership began making phone calls on the public telephones in the lobby area adjacent to the studio. They called newspapers, radio, and other television stations to inform the media that the gay community had shut down KCOP. Not quite true, KCOP did not go off the air. Although we occupied their largest studio, it was not their only one, and modified air life went on for them.

When the news of our occupation began to break throughout Los Angeles, more members of the community rushed to the station. Management shut the gates, informing those of us who were inside that anyone who wanted to could leave. We were also told if we didn't leave, we would be arrested for trespassing. Management then went away. I believe they thought if they left us alone, we would simply be gone in the morning.

Come morning, however, the news of our occupation of the studio was headline. I personally spoke to one television reporter from another station and asked him why so much attention was being paid to our situation. He grinned at me through the wire fence and simply said, "It's a slow news day."

Soon we had more people outside the fence than we had inside. Lesbians and gays alike passed food over the fence, which was greatly appreciated. By the second morning a few industrious people had set up camp stoves and were actually *cooking* us bacon and eggs!

At one point on the second day, station management again gave us an opportunity to leave. There were some lesbians and gays who opted to do so. Maybe they had sensitive jobs and didn't want to risk being arrested, or just weren't committed enough. Who knows? I saw no sign from anyone who stayed that they thought less of those who opted to leave. However, when the guards opened the gate in the wire fence to let them out, other members of the community rushed the gate and got into the station's grounds. By now we had the run of the studio, restrooms, lobby area outside the studio we were in, and the back parking lot.

On the second day a committee was formed to negotiate with the station. It was initiated, of course, by Morris, who was very experienced in protesting. I believe most of the members were those in the studio from the beginning, but I know of at least one who had come in when the gate was rushed. How she got on the committee I don't know, but I for one felt she did not deserve to be there when she was not part of the original protest.

Along with giving us an option to leave that second day, management also reiterated they would have us arrested. Morris, who had been detained before, spoke to us about the possibility of arrest, what it would entail, and gave us instructions on how to handle ourselves. Specifically, he wanted our assurance we would not fight back. He wanted it to be a peaceful sit-in, not a violent action or reaction.

I had never been threatened with arrest before, yet I never hesitated about staying. I was totally enraged that any person could be allowed to advocate my death on television without knowing me and what I stood for. The concept that I should be killed for who I wished to love was simply beyond the pale. Mort Sahl did not speak as if he even considered members of the lesbian/gay community human beings. Considering what heterosexual men have perpetrated throughout history (rape, murder, molestation of children, and unspeakable torture and deprivation), who I choose to go to bed with seems like nothing. More importantly, any person with enough stature to have his or her own television program, has the power to persuade. His words could very well inspire multitudes of sociopaths and psychopaths to increase the beatings and killings in our community, of which there had been far too many already.

The committee called for the station to fire Mort Sahl, but management declared they would not do so under duress, and that point could not be negotiated. Please note, however, that at the end of the season, Sahl's contract was not renewed. On the third day the committee and management came to an agreement and we all went home, tired, hungry and a little smelly. We never saw a police presence. No doubt management could envision the shots on every Los Angeles news program, and maybe even nationally, of lesbian/gay protestors being limply dragged out of their television station. It would not have been a pretty sight and certainly would have reflected their inability to control the situation in their own studio.

Eventually the community did get some programing to counter Sahl's invitation to genocide. Sahl got himself a lot of bad publicity and lost his show. It's doubtful that he ever changed his mind. If he ever reads or hears about my including this episode of his life in my memoirs, he'll probably sue me. So be it, as it would only get him more bad publicity and, at seventy-five and no personal property of any worth, I have nothing to lose. But this disagreeable episode of life did happen, and I was there.

And through it I learned I cared enough about my community to go to jail for it if need be, even if I didn't have to do so on this occasion.

52

Separatism or Self Determination?

The two most controversial subjects in the lesbian community may be the lesbian support of gay men in the AIDS crisis, and the decision to be, or not to be, a separatist.

From a humanitarian point of view *any* epidemic needs to be addressed by everyone: male or female, gay or straight, conservative or liberal, every nationality, every religion. But there was a point where the AIDS crisis lost my support. I can be as sympathetic and concerned as the next person when someone's dying of cancer or rampant pneumonia and there is no cure, only certain death. Remember, at the beginning no one knew what AIDS was or how it was transmitted.

The AIDS virus mutated in and was exported from Africa, parts of which now have infection rates as high as eighty percent. It has nothing to do with homosexuality and both men and women are infected. It is a sexually transmitted disease. But you know all this, along with the fact one infected gay man arrived in the United States and began spreading the virus. Back then nobody, gay or straight, had protected sex. There were, and are, other sexually transmitted diseases (STDs), most of which are curable with antibiotics. Only syphilis carries a death sentence, and that only after thirty or forty years or more.

Unfortunately the sexual practices of many gay men, multiplicity with strangers, spread the AIDS virus quickly throughout gay communities and beyond in our highly mobile society. I don't assign any blame here; people were doing what they always did without major consequences, like death. However after a few years, when the cause and transmission of AIDS became well known, when gay bars offered free condoms and posters urging their use, gay men had the opportunity to change their behavior. Some did. The majority chose to ignore warnings, taking the "it can't happen to me" attitude and continuing their promiscuity.

Gradually AIDS spread into the general community through shared needles, bisexuality, and other interactions. A straight man has sex with an infected gay man outside a bar. He becomes infected and subsequently transmits the disease to a prostitute and his wife, who passes the infection on to her unborn child. From one night's trespass with a gay man, we now have one straight male, two women and one child infected. Unlikely scenario? No, a common one, particularly hard in some communities where men won't use condoms because they're not "manly."

This is not a treatise on AIDS; there are others who could do a much better job than I. It is only an introduction on why I quit supporting the AIDS Project LA and other organizations. At the point where it became obvious to me that the gay male community could have stopped, or greatly reduced, the transmission of AIDS *and chose not to so for their own hedonism*, they lost me, my support, and my donations.

I was once asked to be on a panel with the topic: "Is AIDS a Lesbian Issue?" I was on the side that believed it was not, as there was only a minuscule number of AIDS cases among lesbians, and they had been infected through shared needles and bi-sexuality, not woman to woman sexual encounters. The panel was sponsored by a group respected in our community, so I agreed to participate, knowing their reputation and fairness. When I got there I was blind-sided. I represented one side of the issue, and seven other members of the panel represented the other! I lost a lot of respect for the supposedly "fair minded" sponsors and moderator, but went on anyway, even being outnumbered seven to one.

As the discussion progressed I realized there was a hidden agenda. Some on the panel, who were among the lesbian community's "leaders," and some in the audience of about fifty women, were more concerned about their own personal position in the gay community than the spread of AIDS to lesbians. One prominent "leader" said, "As more of the men die off, we need to be ready to step into their positions."

It appeared to me some of these women were taking the side of making AIDS a lesbian issue in order to increase their visibility in the gay community, with the goal of replacing gay men in leadership positions, which were dominated by men as it has been throughout history. This is not and never has been a goal in my life. My work has always been to empower women without the assistance of men. Has any one besides me noticed the NOW name says "for women," not "of women?" NOW never intended to make the fight for women's rights solely with women's energy. Many lesbian leaders in Los Angeles never intended to gain power through their own resources and hard work, but on the backs of dying AIDS victims. When this is read, there will be a hue and cry of denial. But this is my memory of events and if someone else has a different perspective, let her write them down as I have.

It is my opinion that the only way women will gain any real power, in politics, business, universities, and media presentations, is by bonding together and supporting each other through their own endeavors, not through working with men who, even if gay, have grown up with male privilege and assume their right to command. When it comes to elections, women (who represent more than fifty percent of the voters), don't support women candidates. Many married women tend to vote with their husbands, no matter how anti-woman the male candidate is. Women have been subjugated for so long in history some automatically feel they're not able to make their own sound decisions. As for lesbians, a great portion of them simply have given up and don't vote at all.

Is it better today than yesterday? You bet, and it will be even better tomorrow, whether that means a year, a decade or a generation from now. But until women in general wake up to the realization they already have power by majority effect and decide to seize it for themselves, the process will be two steps forward and one back.

Which brings me to the question: am I a separatist?

If I never had to see, speak to, work with, or acknowledge another man—gay or straight—for the rest of my life, I would be a happy person. I would gladly give up the handful of good men I've known, (both gay and straight), to avoid the worthless ones who have dominated. I guess that makes me a wanna-be separatist. But the fact is, it's not practical. I have learned over my seven decades plus of life to mostly ignore men, or at least deal with them as little as possible. Does that mean all women are perfect? Far from it. Some have taken on the attributes of men that make their behavior nearly identical. I want to believe if they didn't feel they were competing with men, they'd be more woman-like. Science is finding out women really are basically different than men on many levels. I have always believed that to be true.

There is a short story by James Tiptree, Jr (a woman author) entitled, "Houston, Houston, Do You Read?" It takes place in the future when no men are left on Earth and there have been none for several generations. Women are capable of everything that needs to be done, including reproduction without male sperm. The story takes place in a space ship which has encountered an old, derelict ship that has been wandering through time for a couple of hundred years. There are several men aboard, left over from the past, who have been lost in the space-time continuum without aging. The women have to decide whether or not they will rescue the men, members of a past society the women have never experienced, only read about. The story is about the decision, and the interactions between the crews when the rescue has been made and the male astronauts come aboard the all-female ship. Another decision needs to be made with what to do with these men who were raised with male privilege and have entered an all-woman society after they've been rescued. I recommend all women read this short story and contemplate what *you* would have decided under these same circumstances.

53

The Gay/Straight Conflict

As gays and lesbians fight for our rights as human beings, there is an increasing level of conflict between the homosexual and non-homosexual lifestyles. This has always amazed me. I cannot figure out why a person who does not embrace my orientation could care less about what I do in the privacy of my own home. Or whether or not I walk down the street holding hands with another person, any other person. I do them no harm.

I can understand why less intelligent or less educated men might consider me competition for the women of the world, until it is explained to them that such competition does not actually exist. Women who are interested in other women wouldn't choose them anyway. Of course, there is the problem of male *ego*. Because of the way boy children are raised with male privilege, they grow into men believing they are *entitled* to the first choice of everything. Unfortunately for them, it just doesn't work that way in the real world.

As gays and lesbians have become more visible, conflict with non-gays has risen significantly. First we deal with parents, siblings and close friends. You come out of your closet, your mom exclaims "What did I do wrong?" (nothing) and your dad throws you out of the house and never speaks to you again. You gain some civil rights, domestic partnership, and maybe a civil union (let alone the possibility of marriage), and the so-called "christian right" becomes more vitriolic and violent. Why? What harm are we doing to them?

I believe the hue and cry is because of the conflict they are feeling internally. They would most likely deny this because they don't want to look closely at themselves. I have spoken here and there of my own family throughout this manuscript, and I want to do so one more time as an example.

I, too, had parents and siblings, and came out to my mother and sisters. Over many years my mother had upon occasion asked me if I was ever going to get married. Of course she meant to a man. For a long time I looked for a logical opening to tell her I was a lesbian. One day she again asked about marriage and I told her never, as I was a lesbian. Her reaction was: "Oh, I never thought of that." From then forward any women I was with was as welcome in her home as I was. Next I told my sister Anne, the one who raised me as a child. Her reaction was: "Oh, that explains a lot of things."

I don't believe anyone ever told my father and he and I never spoke of it. And, as I mentioned earlier, I never talked with my brother about my being a lesbian, but I was sure he knew. He always treated my partners with respect.

However, I do have one other sister, Virginia, who gave me the name Jinx. She is the example of conflict in my family that I believe reflects the struggle in the general population. Being very religious, she could not justify her love of her baby sister with her belief in her religion. However, about the time Virginia started making me special cards, and even though we were not communicating, she also stopped condemning me for being a lesbian. I see this as an example of conflict between two emotions that only time changed. I call that acceptance. She is as religious today as forty years ago, and I am an outrageous lesbian with national recognition for my service to the community. She could not change me with all her praying and verbal attempts, and I would not have been able to change her religious beliefs if I had attempted to so do.

Now, look at this story from a national conscience point of view. Multiply my sister by the tens of millions of parents and siblings and friends who are conflicted by their personal emotions. All right, some of them really hate gays and lesbians, and some of them really don't care one way or the other. But in between are the majority who hold the "love the person but hate the act" position which is very difficult to process. I believe time is the answer to settle this struggle. Be out there, take your place in society, and be proud of who you are. If that happens to be a lesbian, so be it. It won't be in my lifetime, but I am absolutely sure this conflict will go away with time. It is the newness of it that creates the problems. I can honestly say I have seen a sea-change in attitudes in the more than fifty years I have been totally out of my closet. Because conditions change so much faster now, you'll experience an equal change in attitude in the next twenty years or less.

As a post script to this section, I find it extremely disappointing that the "Christian Right" is the leader in opposition to my existence. Members of that contingent have said all their objections are in the Bible. Not only are they quoting the Old Testament, but they seem to forget the Old Testament was handed down verbally for generation after generation before being committed to the written word. You've all been to parties where a story is whispered around from person to person and at the end, both the beginning story and last version are told out loud. They are hardly the same tale at all, changed by mis-communication, biases of the teller, and embellishment. That is exactly how the Old Testament was created.

More importantly, Christians are supposed to be those whose religion is based upon the teachings of Jesus Christ, not the Old Testament. Jesus taught compassion, forgiveness and love. Jesus supported the concept that all men and women were equal and worthy. He did not embrace hate, or beating/killing someone because of who they are, or even belittling a person for their beliefs. I cannot imagine Jesus' reaction to those who joined the Crusades, or condoned the Inquisition, in his name. If he wouldn't put up with money changers in the Temple, what would he have thought about the Medici dynasty and the present priest child abusers, let alone those who have broken the First Commandment: Tho Shalt Not Kill, by blowing up doctors and abortion clinics?

I am of no religion and I cannot possibly accept the acts of those calling themselves "Christians" who do not follow the teachings of Jesus Christ. What hypocrisy!

Or maybe religion just doesn't appeal to me.

PART 7

THE LATER YEARS

54

Alicia and Fantasies Unlimited

Alicia joined the Lesbian Rights Task Force the last year I participated with them (1979). Frankly I didn't notice her much at the beginning. After a while she began to join a handful of us who trooped a couple of blocks up the street after meetings to a coffee shop for ice cream, dessert, or coffee. It was through those monthly get-togethers I began to know her better. After dating for a year or so, we ended up being domestic partners for the next twenty-three and a half years.

She may have been quiet, but she sure was and is talented. She had a regular job in the medical field as a cytotechnologist, but for a while Alicia failed to mention to me she was also an artist. I found out about that side of her when she was approaching a deadline for illustrating a book and when I visited her house I saw all those pictures spread out on a drawing table. She specifically illustrated short stories and books in the fantasy genre, like in "fantasy and science fiction."

Eventually she took me with her to a Fantasy & Science Fiction Convention where I discovered she was a celebrity, having won many awards for her artwork and being published in an ever-expanding list of magazines and books. She also had a volume of her own early artwork out as well. Alicia would sell her original artwork, relatively inexpensively, in the convention's art show where entered work was bid upon by her fans.

As Alicia showed me around the convention, introducing me and giving attention to her adoring fans, I kept hearing one thing over and over. Her followers would say to her, "I love your work, but I can't afford it." I had recently been laid off from UCLA after eighteen years, and was unemployed. My brain started clicking. If they liked her work, but couldn't afford her originals (even though they sold at modest prices from ten dollars to a couple of hundred for more complex illustrations), there had to be something else.

Prints! I have always loved books and art and theater. I already knew about signed/number limited editions, and it seemed to me to be a way Alicia's fans could own an image of her wonderful art.

Thus Fantasies Unlimited was born. The first convention at which I sold her work I offered about a dozen black and white reproductions for five dollars each. They were relatively simple 8 1/2x11" pictures, signed and numbered limited to an edition of 100. They were highly received. Fans were thrilled about the availability of her images, and we sold several hundred dollars worth on our first outing.

Over the next fifteen years Fantasies Unlimited was my job. We created a legal business which lasted for twenty years before the recession of the mid-1990's did it in. After all, if you've lost your job and are having a difficult time feeding your family, you don't buy artwork, even if it feeds your soul. Additionally, by this time Alicia was getting tired, and wanted a reprieve, only working her full time regular job.

For my part, I ran the business, served as her agent, and took on most of the jobs around the house to allow her time to draw. I also drove all over the United States, many times alone, setting up a booth and selling her art prints and associated art on note cards, t-shirts, books, rubber stamps and coloring portfolios. I can honestly say that even though it was hard work, I was so proud of Alicia's talents it was fun to offer her images to her fans. I didn't really have to sell it; it sold itself while I stood by to answer questions and take their money.

Essentially both Alicia and I worked two jobs, although typical for our society, my taking care of the household (shopping and cooking, doing laundry, paying bills and doing the banking, etc), didn't count as much in Alicia's eyes. For first few years of our relationship, I also published the LN.

It was true I had no way to accurately predict how much would sell at any particular convention. If Alicia was there, say when she was invited as the convention's Artist Guest of Honor (GOH), I knew we would sell three to four times as much as when I went to the convention alone. It also depended what city we were in. For example we did well in Seattle, but never well in Portland, whether Alicia attended or not. This was a business with the intent to make a profit. Expenses were based on location, size of the convention which dictated how big a booth we had to rent, and hotel expenses. The latter was always paid by the convention when Alicia was GOH. When she wasn't GOH, I'd stay in the least expensive motel in the area and sleep in the van while on the road.

Monetarily the worst convention I worked was a first-time, very small show held locally, which meant I was able to go home each night and sleep in my own bed. Even though expenses were low, I only broke even. The best convention money-wise was in San Francisco where Alicia was GOH for the World Science Fiction Convention. We sold twelve thousand dollars of her artwork in five days, and it was all profit as the convention picked up all the expenses for her being there.

I write about this memory with fondness. Without a doubt it was the second best job of my life, UCLA being the best. It was with regret on my part, (but not Alicia's), that after twenty years we officially closed the business down. A couple of observations about my work history:

> - - - I tend to stay in the same place for a long time if possible:
> 16 years in the Air Force and AF Reserve,
> 14 years publishing *The Lesbian News*,
> 20 years selling fantasy art, and as I write this,
> 12 years and counting on my current job
>
> .
>
> - - - I tend to get associated with talented people and work to promote them:
> BLS Photo with Wendy, based on her wonderful Thoroughbred photography,
> Fantasies Unlimited with Alicia, based on her exquisite award-winning art.

It's not that I don't have my own talents. I was supervising a hundred and twenty-five women in the Air Force when I was twenty years old, and a crew of men in the reserves when I was still in my twenty's. I was very successful in my research job at UCLA where I was supervisor of the Driving Simulation Laboratory. I accomplished *The Lesbian News* with volunteer assistance. I managed a full time business of art sales. I'm highly respected on my current job, being offered (and turned down) the opportunity to become a supervisor. Been there, done that, no longer needed to prove myself.

I would evaluate myself as being highly proficient in organization and administration, a feat many think impossible for themselves. I've never met a job I couldn't do, although I know they exist. I simply don't put myself into a position in the work place I can't handle.

Relationships, however, are another story altogether! I actually thought I'd finally got it "right" with Alicia. We spent nearly a quarter of a century knowing each other, dating, and living together. Unfortunately I grew older, have some medical problems left over from a major illness, as well as arthritis consistant with my age. I'm certainly not the physical person I was in my forties or fifties. Soon after my seventieth birthday she informed me she had found someone else, a person twenty years younger than I was. If there was some other reason she broke off our relationship after all those years, she never told me of it. Unfortunately we did not part as friends. It was a good run and I'm not too surprised it ended. I just wish she had done so in a more honest manner so we could have remained friends as I have with other ex-lovers.

55

Cheating Death or Just Wanting to Live?

I had been working at Department of Water & Power less than a year when I came home from work one evening, had a late dinner, and shortly thereafter doubled over with the worst pain I had ever experienced. My partner rushed me to the emergency room where they filled me with pain medication and essentially knocked me out while they did tests. My partner held my durable power of attorney for decision making; I was totally unconscious.

As a DWP part-time employee I had no benefits. That means no health insurance. I had not had any health insurance for the past twenty years since I was laid off at UCLA. I had always been a very healthy person and was holding out for Medicare as I couldn't afford insurance premiums working only part time. I was a couple of years short of sixty-five.

I woke up for a minute in an ambulance, and later for about five minutes in a bed in some hospital room. I have virtually no memory of the next month! When I finally did gain enough consciousness to be cognizant of my surroundings, I found I was in Olive View Hospital in Sylmar, a county hospital which is also a teaching facility for the UCLA Medical School. Without insurance or medicare, no regular hospital would admit me. Fortunately my partner was aware that Olive View was rated as the best of the county facilities and she successfully argued to have me transferred there.

I was put into a medically induced coma for nine days, intubated and fitted with a Foley (a catheter for urination). I was later told the only part of me working on its own was my heart. I was in the Intensive Care Unit (ICU) for six weeks. You think of post-operative patients being in ICU for two or three days. When my mother had a heart attack, she was in ICU five days. I was there six *weeks*! After bringing me out of the coma, I was heavily medicated with morphine for the next three weeks wherein I can only remember fleeting moments and hallucinations.

I was diagnosed with an extreme case of gall bladder-pancreatitis. It seems I had gall stones (which I did not know about, having no symptoms of gall stones until I doubled over with pain), and a stray stone had wandered from its path and blocked the common duct it shares with pancreatic secretions just before entering the intestine. This may be more anatomy that you want to know.

However, I was told, the pancreas is a very sensitive organ and upon blockage began to inflame from the backed up secretions. When it became severely infected, it let me know dramatically. To fight the infection I volunteered (?) to be part of a drug study for a new antibiotic. I'll never know if I received the new drug or an old one already in use (no placebos here), but I started to get better.

After about three weeks I went to surgery to have my gall bladder removed and, five days later, went back to surgery to have my abdomen cleaned out and part of my pancreas removed. I was told later they removed about two liters of pus and necrotic material. Picture a big two-liter soda bottle's worth of gunk. My question is this: when the surgeon was in there taking out the gall bladder, why didn't she look around to see what else needed to be handled? Removing the gall bladder required only small incisions. When they came back to debride the pancreas, they slit me along my rib cage from one side to the other. I took two months to heal in a very painful "wet to dry" procedure (no external stitches). I wasn't healed when I left the hospital so my partner had to play doctor twice a day for a month changing my bandages.

Being a teaching hospital, I was seen by a team of a resident and several interns. I gather this team came by every day to see my progress. I have no memory of them until about the fifth week when my medication was reduced and I was cognizant of most things going on around me. Not that I could communicate verbally. When I woke up I had this hole in my throat below my larynx and an air tube hooked up to it. Apparently I had so much trouble breathing and receiving enough oxygen on my own when they tried to remove me from intubation, I gave the doctors permission to do a tracheostomy so I could survive.

To this day I am amazed that the hospital was able to get "informed consent" from me, and on several occasions had me sign release forms for surgery, when I was not fully conscious. I can't believe any consent or legitimate signature given under circumstances where a patient is under such high medication and not cognizant of the surrounding circumstances, would hold up in a court of law as being legal. But do I care? Hell no! I'm here aren't I?

One day after I was well on my way to recovery and about to be moved from the ICU, one of the doctors on my team stopped by my bedside alone. He smiled at me and told me when the team had first processed me the night I arrived, they had predicted seventy-five percent mortality. That means they gave me a one in four chance to live. Due to the tube in my throat I couldn't comment, but I don't think he expected me to. He smiled again and walked away. It was the only time in the six weeks I was in ICU a doctor from the team spoke directly to me. Only the surgeon had talked to me personally, and most of the nurses with whom I had daily contact, who were really great.

One particular nurse saw to it a I received a very fancy, special (and expensive) bed. Not only did it have a pulsating mattress, it had a built in scale to weigh me on a regular basis, and could be manipulated into various positions, including one in which I was sitting up practically like a chair. Thanks to that bed, which the hospital rented just for me, I never had a bed sore, even though I didn't leave the bed for seven weeks. Only my last week in the hospital, finally out of ICU, was I put into a regular hospital bed.

When I was struck down with pancreatitis, not only did my partner take care of me, but so did all my immediate extended lesbian family. I'm told that within hours of being admitted to Olive View, the waiting room was full of my friends waiting for news and supporting my partner. I'm also told that while I was in a coma, each would come to visit me as they could, sit by my bedside, and talk to me. Nurses told them it was believed a person in a coma still had some realization of those around and could possibly hear them, if not respond. There may be some proof of this. Of course I was hooked up to every possible monitor. I was told by friends who saw it happen that they would be by my side talking to me, but when my partner arrived, touched my forehead and told me she was there, they witnessed a drop in my blood pressure on the monitor.

After I regained consciousness and was more aware of my surroundings, some of my extended family would come to read to me or just visit, until the last week. Seven years after all this happened I no longer have my partner, and only two of those women are still my friends. Life happens when you least expect it, and there's nothing you can do about it. I look at it this way: these women were in my life when I needed them most, and without a doubt helped save me. Now I'm much stronger, and although I miss some of them, I can survive without them.

The major problem with being flat on your back for seven weeks is that you lose muscle tone despite the in-bed exercises you attempt to do. A week after I left ICU for a regular double occupancy room, a physical therapist showed up with a helper and said, "It's time you walk." They swung my legs over the side of the bed, took an arm on each side, and pulled me up to my feet. I promptly fell flat on my face. Well, no, I didn't fall, but only because these two women held me up. I could not even stand; my knees wouldn't lock. They put me back to bed and told me not to worry. They would be back the next day and I *would* walk.

The next day they showed up as promised, got me out of bed and with their assistance I not only stood, but walked three steps and back! The third day they brought a walker with them and they showed me how to use it. They also showed Alicia how to hold me up from falling by wrapping a sheet around me under my arms to give me balance. This was the day before the Thanksgiving holiday. Finally the physical therapist informed us they were off for the next four days, my partner could help me walk, and she'd see me the following Monday!

There were two conditions for my being released by the hospital to go home. First, I had to be able to inhale enough oxygen to have a ninety percent saturation reading. By now I had a smaller tube in my throat that I could hold my finger over to block and then be able to talk. I had started talking again about two weeks before. But I wasn't breathing on my own deeply enough to sustain sufficient oxygen. About the same time I started learning to walk again, the tube came out of my throat, although I had supplemental oxygen available. I started exercising my lungs with a device with a ping pong ball. Breath deeply enough, the ball reaches the top of the device. I started out barely able to get it off the bottom. A week later I easily zipped it to the top.

The second condition was I had to be able to move with the walker well enough to get from my bed to the bathroom and back. By the time the physical therapist visited me on Monday after Thanksgiving, only four days later, I could get myself out of the bed, walk out of the room (with the walker) and down the hall and back, and get myself back into bed without assistance! She was surprised and pleased. In three more days I was walking around the nurses' station twice without resting. I could indeed get myself to the bathroom, if not too rapidly.

Two days later I was released from the hospital, two months after I had arrived. I hadn't cried in those two months, but my eyes filled with tears when I was pushed out the front door in a wheel chair and I saw sunlight. It was the first time in two months I actually believed I was going to get out of the hospital alive.

I continued recovery for an additional two months, beginning with a wheel chair/walker, graduating to walker alone, and finally to a cane. I was off work four months. Remember, I was well past the guaranteed six months promised when I was hired and they did not have to hold the job for me. But they did. They were very good to me, easing me into the work period. I was supposed to work 5 hours a day; the first day I worked two and was exhausted. It took me another month of recovery to get rid of the cane and then slowly I got better and better.

I was warned by the doctor upon release that there would be consequences from the illness; probably permanent. Indeed my less than whole pancreas does not produce either enough enzymes for proper digestion, or enough insulin to control blood sugar levels within normal range. Therefore I take additional digestive enzymes daily and, after complete recovery, have had no problems with my digestive tract. I am now diabetic and must test daily and take pills to spur insulin creation, as well as taking a long-release insulin at bedtime. So long as I watch what I eat, I'm able to keep my blood sugar levels within an acceptable range and most of the time within normal range.

I did have one frustrating consequence from my pancreatic surgery which no one anticipated. About a year after the surgery in the hospital, it was discovered I had a pancreatic pseudo-cyst. Secretions from the pancreas were leaking out instead of going into my intestinal track as they normally would do. Where the pancreas had been cut away, and a membrane formed over the cut area, the secretions pushed out the membrane creating a sac in my abdomen. The sac grew to fill all available space in the abdomen, pushing kidneys, liver and stomach as far as it could. If that sac had broken, I most likely would have died from peritonitis. My regular doctor discovered it in a routine annual physical.

In the next three years I would ultimately undergo three surgeries to correct the pseudo-cyst (it's why they call it "practicing medicine"), the third procedure being the one I should have had in the first place. So due to the initial gall stone slipping out of place, I underwent five surgeries in five years and got very tired of hospitals. The good news is the last procedure has worked beautifully and I appear to be good to go for the rest of my life so long as I handle the diabetes. It has been quite an experience and one I wish not to repeat.

56

My Desire To Be a Writer

I mentioned previously that I began to write poetry before I was seven years old. That was only the beginning! "Writing" has flowed from me one way or another throughout my life.

At UCLA I wrote both preliminary and final research papers, even though my supervisor's name appeared on them as author. No problem, that's what I got paid to do and it was commonplace. For the fourteen years I owned and published the LN I not only edited literally everything that graced its pages, I also wrote original material and a column for a while. Both UCLA and the LN were non-fiction.

Except for the poetry, my first venture into fiction was a short story I wrote after starting back to college after the Air Force. That was at Pasadena City College. I entered a story in their annual literary contest for students. It won a blue ribbon, although I did not attend the ceremony and didn't benefit directly from any adoration of my writing skills. By the way, the story was a mystery.

Like at least half the population of the world, I always wanted to be a writer. I just wasn't very specific about what kind of a writer, thus the thirty years I spent writing non-fiction. However, soon after winning at PCC, I began writing my first novel. Not a mystery, but the life story of a lesbian born in the mid-west. I'm still writing it, fifty years later, having spent long periods of time letting it rest while I was doing other things. I have written about one hundred and fifty pages and have taken my protagonist from her first day of school into her late twenties. Who knows? Maybe I'll actually finish it before I die just to satisfy myself.

Meanwhile during those fifty years, I've completed more than a dozen short stories covering fantasy, mystery and one young adult story with a Native American theme. Two short story mysteries have been published in

Sisters-in-Crime/LA anthologies. I've also completed two novelettes (one a mystery with a lesbian protagonist and the other a lesbian "breaking up" story), and have a third lesbian novel (mystery) about three-quarters done. Of course, right now I'm writing my autobiography. When I finish the bio, my next project is to complete the last novel. *Then* maybe I'll go back to the original fifty-year-old novel and complete it.

It seems all my life I've found something to do which, at the moment, felt more important than writing my own stuff. I put every other project ahead of my writing. I certainly am a writer, but maybe I never really had the passion necessary to be an "author."

Through my thirties, forties, fifties, when I was writing short stories, I also was submitting them here and there for publication. They were always rejected, although I received a hand-written note on a *Redbook* rejection notice that said, "Try us again." Of course, I never did. I've been rejected twice by the lesbian press for the two novelettes (different publishes), and probably rightly so. I can say with confidence, however, writing those pieces was good practice. I really believe the mystery I'm near completing is much better written. When it's finished and edited, I'll most likely try to get it published. I'm a glutton for punishment.

The good news is that after all these years, and now that I'm older and single, I actually have more leisure time. I have no extensive obligations in the community or to any person or animal. Finally, now that I'm in my seventies and only working one job for only a few more months before retiring, I may actually have time to write more!

57

The Attempt At Lesbian Short Fiction

I have always loved reading short stories. It is satisfying to me to be able to sit down and read to the conclusion of a story within an hour or two. Not every reader, nor every writer, shares this love, but many do. It was a dream of mine for a long time to edit a magazine or book of lesbian themed short stories. Please note here, my desire was to be editor, nothing more.

I had the opportunity to mention this once to a prominent lesbian writer, and she suggested she might know of a person who would financially support such a project. She put me and a potential publisher in touch with each other. To make a long story a little shorter, suffice it to say we came to a verbal agreement and I started working, without a contract, on the launch of *Lesbian Short Fiction (LSF)* in a trade paper format.

First off I contacted every lesbian bookstore I could get an address for and asked them to post an enclosed flyer asking for submissions. I sent this request world-wide. The basic rules were: 1) it must have a lesbian theme, 2) it must be written in English, and 3) it could be no longer than five thousand words (around twenty double spaced, typed pages). The call for submissions did not restrict the gender or sexuality of the writer, only the material, and we did end up with a couple of men being accepted.

Manuscripts started arriving slowly, gradually picking up speed as the word spread. Most of the stories, as is true of the "slush pile" for any publication in the world, were not of a quality to be printed. I created a check-off list, an idea I got from writer/publisher Marion Zimmer Bradley's rejection notice, and began notifying writers. I detailed enough about the story to assist the writer to know why I was rejecting it for publication, including writing personal notes on the back of the form. I also suggested to some that with a bit of re-writing, it might be accepted. I'm happy to say that several women did re-write and re-submit, and were published.

It took a while to accumulate enough stories for the first, Premiere, issue which published in Spring, 1996. The tales in the first issue weren't as even as later issues, but I believe all were quite acceptable. We had much less to choose from at the beginning, and could be more selective after we started rolling. It was the intent that *LSF* be a quarterly publication, but that never happened.

From the beginning I had trouble with the publisher. She was under the impression that all she had to do was supply the printing costs; all I ever intended was to be editor. It is traditionally the publisher's job to actually put the book together and distribute it. As it turned out, I attempted to do everything except pay the printing fees. Unfortunately, what I didn't have was distribution knowledge, which is the key to success. I dealt directly with each bookstore, many of which never got around to paying their bills, and some of which went out of business.

As Issue 2 was being printed in the Fall of 1996, six months after the first issue, I was admitted to the hospital with the near death experience I detailed in Chapter 55 and was not able to distribute or work on *LSF* for many months. I could not publish Issue 3 until the Fall, 1997, one year later. Whatever momentum we had quickly disappeared. I limped along for the next couple of years putting out one issue in 1998 and the last issue in 1999, with little support from the publisher.

Except for my personal relationships, I have always expected my endeavors to be successful, and they have been. *Lesbian Short Fiction* is my first and only failure. Not that each issue published wasn't my best effort, but I was not able to expand it into a quarterly publication with a continuing readership. I still believe the concept of a book of lesbian short fiction is a good idea and can be a beginning for new, exciting writers, as well as entertaining for readers. But my personal lesson was simple: I can't do it by myself.

The Lesbian News succeeded because I had a team of women assisting with every issue. *Lesbian Short Fiction* failed because I had no team and no distribution assistance. If I had it to do over again, I would have contacted an existing lesbian publisher to see if they were interested in the project under their monogram, with me as editor. Oh, well, hindsight is wonderful, isn't it?

58

My Last Job!

When the recession of the mid 1990s hit, and Alicia started to wear out from her heavy production, art sales dropped dramatically. It became apparent I needed to look for another job. Not an easy task when you're in your sixties. Potential employers cannot discriminate by law due to your age, but they find other reasons not to hire you. I always love the "over qualified" excuse. I also had little practical job experience to fall back on. Yes, I'd been in "retail sales" for the previous twenty years, but selling fantasy art does not translate well into traditional sales positions. Frankly, sales was never a field I ever wanted to work in anyway and I never considered selling Alicia's wonderful artwork as "sales.".

I had spent eighteen years at UCLA and felt comfortable looking for a job there, but it was a very different job atmosphere all those years later. I had been relatively young the first time around and started in an entry position of Laboratory Assistant I. I was laid off as a Lab Asst IV! At sixty years old, they weren't looking at me for an entry level position. They weren't enthusiastic about placing me, even if they couldn't tell me to go away and leave them alone.

I knew three women who were employed by the Los Angeles Department of Water and Power. One day I received a telephone call from the one who was in a supervisory position telling me I needed to fill out an application for employment *that day!* DWP was looking to hire some part-timers with no benefits and no guarantee of a job beyond six months. They were not going outside the company (which would have generated hundreds of applicants), but were accepting applications from family and friends of employees. These were not civil service jobs, so that was legal. My friend told me I would also have to interview and, although she could get me the interview, I was on my own thereafter. The positions were for Customer Service Representatives in the Collections Department. What did I know about collections? But it was a chance at a job, so I interviewed. As it turned out they hired about fifteen reps out of thirty applications. I was one of them. Strange hours (early afternoon to early evening), guaranteed for six months only, and no benefits. Twelve years later I'm still there, full time, partial benefits and good work hours.

After a three week training course, I was dumped on a telephone to deal with customers who can't or won't pay their water and power bills. My job was to get them to do so in a timely manner. After a while I began to realize that ninety-five percent or more of the DWP's customers pay their bill on time. The other five percent are the ones I talk to over and over again. I started this job believing everyone tells the truth. After all, I did. But the third time a person tells me his/her mother "just died and I have to go back East for the funeral," you begin to wonder. Most customers don't seem to realize we keep notes on their accounts. Now I know there are some people who have no qualms about lying, if it will get their bill postponed.

Eventually I was hired full time, Collections was merged with the Customer Call Center, and I'm hanging on accumulating time toward retirement. I'm aiming for thirty years. I'm too old to actually work that long for DWP, I'd be in my nineties, but I've been able to purchase or "buy back" my "other government service" time: Air Force, State of California (UCLA), and part-time LA City. At the end of 2006 I had 28 years accumulated. The question I had to deal with then was whether working two more years was worth the difference in retirement pay. It was, so I am. I'll be seventy five when I retire, which will still beat my dad by five years!

This is definitely my last job! It is also the *worst* job I ever held, even though it pays the best. They can't fire me for my age (I'm the oldest rep in the Call Center but not the oldest person working for DWP), they can't discriminate against me for being a lesbian, or wearing short hair and no bra, and I'm working only four days a week. The problem is not the job itself, but management which doesn't appear to have anyone on staff who can assist them with the psychology of dealing with workers in a stress-filled occupation. I used to think the higher up you went in government, the less efficient procedures were. I've changed my mind. Having been in the military (federal government service), at UCLA (state government service), and LADWP (city government service), the last is the least effective. I like the people I work with, even the supervisors, but many procedures are illogical, repressive and inefficient. Not that I've written here anything I haven't said in person and out loud!

CONCLUSION

I've come to the end of my memoir. Either I have died or I have ceased to have anything new worth writing about. I have updated and added a bit to my autobiography in the year I've taken to write the manuscript. The fact is, I really don't expect much of value to occur to me any longer. I think I accomplished what I set out to do: write about the occurrences of my life I feel would enlighten the reader as to who I am and how I got here.

If you've perused the entire manuscript you know it is not an expose of my sexual prowess (or lack thereof). I have mentioned the women I had significant relationships with, and I've revealed as much of our interactions as I believe necessary to prove their influence in my life. Technically I suppose every woman I ever slept with, or was refused by, or interacted with, added something to my life. I still remember nearly all of those moments, but could not include them here. If you should be a person who would fall into this category and weren't mentioned, I'm sorry. However it's my life story and memories important to me matter here.

I had many non-sexual "relationships" with hundreds of women in our lesbian community also. I've not written about them in the most part because whether those were positive or negative interactions, I didn't feel they were significant to my personal growth. I count most of those women as important to my life at the moment, but not in the long term. I have hundreds of wonderful memories of people and events that I just didn't have space for in this manuscript. And if truth be told, I've had a handful of people and occurances I just didn't want to include.

If in my story-telling it appears there are lesbians, or women willing to have a lesbian experience, on every street corner, there are. We are everywhere. We may be invisible to those who don't want to see us. We may be discounted because we are women. But it is my opinion that more women are realizing they don't need men in the same way society has led them to believe in the past. There are simply no jobs that *can't* be done without a male except reproduction. With experimentation in cloning and parthenogenesis progressing rapidly, that one need may soon fall by the wayside. Ironically it will probably be some male trying to immortalize himself that will make the major parthenogenic breakthrough that will lead to his decline. If nothing else, I predict that our society will increasingly separate itself into a female/ male dichotomy with less interaction between the two. Is this science fiction? Flash Gordon's spaceship and flying to the moon was once science fiction, and look what can be done now.

As I said at the very beginning, I have no idea if more than a handful of people will ever read this. If that turns out to be true, it's all right. I wrote this manuscript partially for them and mostly for myself and what little family I have. I have been blessed. Starting in a dysfunctional lower middle class family, I pulled myself up with little emotional support and no financial support. Off to the Air Force earning assistance to go to college. Earning my BA and getting the UCLA job. Publishing the LN and receiving accolades for that. Being out of my lesbian closet since I was twenty two years old in 1956 and pretty much doing things my way. Can't complain.

The year 2006 was particularly rewarding. My second fictional short story was published, I was included in Lillian Faderman and Stuart Timmons' *Gay LA: A History of Sexual Outlaws, Power Politics, and Lipstick Lesbians*, and I was listed as one of about three dozen women from the Southern California area in *Feminists Who Changed America: 1953-1975*, by Barbara Love.

I regret I'm ending my life alone after a twenty-five year relationship that ended when I was seventy years old. It would have been nice to have a companion in the last years of my life, but it (apparently) wasn't meant to be. I find myself relieved I no longer have those responsibilities inherent in a relationship that would become more difficult to accomplish physically as I grow older, like keeping up the yard and hanging holiday lights.

I leave you with this final thought: for everyone to become free to be whoever they want, without discrimination or prejudice holding them back from their goals in life, it is necessary to participate in winning that freedom. Don't expect to hang back and let other people accomplish for you what you do not have the courage to gain for yourself. If the world does not know you exist, how can it be sympathetic to your cause? If your neighbor does not know you're a lesbian, how can you expect her to learn that you share common interests and have overlapping concerns?

I believe I've converted many neighbors and co-workers from negative feelings about lesbians to at least neutral and mostly positive opinions. They have been able to experience me personally, and change their concept of what a lesbian is and what rights we should be afforded. I know I can count them in the hundreds over fifty years of being an open lesbian. There is also no doubt in my mind those converts have influenced their friends, family and acquaintances. It's called a snowball effect, and it really works.

I've done my best for the lesbian community and for my country, and I've done it openly. Hope you can join me.

POEMS

NURSERY RHYMES (Written age 5-8)

The Ship I Saw

I saw a ship go out to sea.
How beautiful it looked to me.
I could not see her sailors;
I could not see her mast.
But I could hear her Captain shout:
"Hey there! Avast!"

The Old Fisherman's Shanty

Down by the shore, down by the sea
an old fisherman's shanty stands.
The sailor, old, sits in the lee
and on the yellow sands.

He sits by the rickety shack bent low
as the waves roll on the shore.
He knows that future days he'll go
a'fishin' nevermore.

Cockadoodledoo

Cockadoodledee the cat ran up the tree.
Cockadoodledoo he had a wonderful view.

Cockadoodledee the cat came down the tree.
Cockadoodledoo he lost his wonderful view.

A Song

Oh what a merry song is this
of ants and bees and little fish,
of leaves a-flying all around
and birds that sing without a sound.

A Song #2

Oh what a joyful song; we sing it all day long.
We're happy all the time. Now tell me, does this rhyme?

I hope it does, you see, for all is lost with me
if rhyme this song does not, they'll put me in a pot!

And if I do not toil, the water they will boil.
And if I have bad reasoning, they'll even put in seasoning!

Birds, Bugs and Dew

The birds are singing in the trees.
The bugs are eating grass.
The dew is sparkling on the leaves
like tiny bits of glass.

The Radio

I'm listening to the radio, it's flattening all the huts.
Of all the banging that is there it should have blown its nuts.
Jumping Jive and Boogie Woogie sure has took the day.
And my ear drums are a'hoping it's not here to stay!

YOUNG POEMS

In The Morning (age 7)

I heard the wind blowing at the break of day.
I heard a train's whistle far, far away.
I heard the birds singing as I lay in bed.
I heard a rooster crowing out in the shed.
I heard mother's footsteps and the door that she shut.
I heard mother calling, "Get up, get up!"

Summertime (age 11)

In the meadow, in the sunshine where the yellow daises grow.
Where blue larkspur sway so gently when the morning breezes blow.
You'll find buttercups a-blooming, delphiniums, lupin fair,
Indian paintbrush, hollyhock and golden poppies everywhere.
Where the insects come to linger, butterflies lite here and there.
All the world is bright and happy for summertime is finally here.

Birds in Spring (age 17)

Among the thick and tangled brush I hear the chirping of a thrush.
And way a-top the sloping hill a bluejay screeching loud and shrill.

A robin sings with all its might on this warm summer's day so bright.
A coo-coo as a small clock's chime never fails to tell the time.

And all the birds, as nature blessed, are always neat and brightly dressed.
For everywhere, on foot or wing, never will they cease to sing.

Birds (age 14)

Brown birds, blue birds, birds with marks of red
streaked among the feathers of their wings and head

Even striped along their tail or on their tiny breast.
Always sprucing up themselves so they look their best.

Sometimes soaring up on high, sometimes on the nest.
Sometimes singing gleeful songs. Each one does his best.

Little birds hatch out a last, keep Ma and Pa a-going,
finding tender bugs and worms to keep their babies growing.

Baby birds grow up quite fast. Then they learn to fly.
Leave their nest and home for good. Go singing in the sky.

The Bells (age 16)

Up in a tower far away I hear them toll the bells.
The bells, they sweetly seem to sway, first soft, and then loud swells.

Ringing there with all their might they sing a wondrous song
of hopes and wishes shining bright. They ring there all day long.

Then when the lonely night creeps up they ring so softly instead.
Until it's time to feed the pup and march off to my bed.

And slower and slower yet they go 'til they cease to swing and sway.
And then night so silent grows as they slowing fade away.

Two Great Rivers of China (age 12)

(Co-written by Jean Beers, Lyria Carranza and Patricia Rae
as a school project.)

There are two great rivers in China, flowing along their beds.
One is call the great Yangzte Kiang, the other the Hwang Ho instead.

The Chinese call Hwang Ho the "Sorrow" which floods its banks in the
spring.
And hundreds of thousands of people go down in its depths, sad thing.

The greatest of all is the Yangzte. You can hear her monotonous roar
across the broad sheet of brown water on the banks of the opposite shore.

Junks and sampans sail on these rivers carrying their cargos of tea.
Also they carry cotton and rice, sailing on out to the sea.

But all these junks and sampans which down these rivers sail
are constantly in danger of rapids that sink their ships, but sometimes fail.

The cities that lay on the Yangtze, the most important at least,
are Chunking and Hankow and Nanking, and when they reach Shanghai,
they cease.

Long Ago (age 12)

The early men of long ago talked together with their hands.
Soon messages sent by beacon fires were used to talk to other bands.
Then the tom-toms sent their calls out to tribesmen far away.
Next came runner's, swift and strong, carrying messages night and day.
Trees were blazed to show the way through forests deep and dark.
Stones were piled or twigs were laid, the trail to clearly mark.

Little Elves (age 16)

Little Elves run and play
and are so happy all the day,
with little suits of brown and green
so as they play they can't be seen
hiding among the leaves and grass.
They're careful of every lad or lass
that might be walking in the glen
not looking 'round for little men.
They do up all their work right quick
and don't pretend that they are sick.
They sing and whistle all day long
and know just every happy song.
They work and play with all their might
until they go to bed at night.
And there they dream of skates and bikes
and taking trips and big long hikes.
For Elves, you see, are just like you
and dream of things most children do.
So go to sleep my little ones
and dream of having lots of fun.
Don't forget tomorrow'll bring
another day of this warm spring
for you to play among yourselves,
just like all the Little Elves.

Crabby Moon (age 17?)

The yellow moon a'sailing cross the sky one night peeked out,
and pushing 'side some fleecy clouds he suddenly did shout,

"Hey there you clouds! Why do you hide my beauty from the all.
I'll have you know that you've no right to stay there like a wall.

"You come around to mar the clear and blueness of the sky.
Well answer me my fleecy ones, come on and tell me why."

The pretty clouds cared not what Mister Moon there had to say.
They just ignored him one and all, and swiftly floated 'way.

For Mister Moon was always spouting 'bout his view and such.
And nothing that he ever said was even thought of much.

For who was Mister Moon to say where fleecy clouds should stray?
He only had one narrow strip on which _he_ had to stay.

So pretty clouds kept floating on and ne'er a word said they.
And wherever frosty wind led, it was there they'd play.

Day and Night (age 17)

(_Alternatively titled: "Insignificant Time."_

A day is but a drop of water from the sea of eternity..

And a night but a star from the endless universe.

HOLIDAY POEMS

Easter Bunny (age 15)

Easter Bunny's come to town,
he'll be here just one day.
He's busy and he hasn't time
to talk or stop to play.
He's coloring eggs all different ways,
blue, yellow, red, and green.
And hiding them in many places
where they can't be seen
by all the little boys and girls
who'll find them in their nests.
He watches them a little while
as behind some grass he rests.
He's thinking as he smiles real big
and slowly hops away,
That he is glad that he can be
back here next Easter day.

Halloween (age 19)

Frosty apples, stalks of corn.
Mr Pumpkin with a scorn
carved upon his yellow face.
Costumed ladies draped in lace.

Jack-O-Lanterns, skeletons,
all to scare the little ones.
Horns and masks and gaiety
for all, from four to sixty three.

"Trick or Treat!" the young one's cry.
Best you never pass them by
else you'll find your hat a-miss,
saved with but a candy kiss.

On this night with spooks a-prowling,
cats "meow" and dogs are howling,
witches potions are a-brewing.
Wonder what that one is stewing?

Better keep your eyes a-leering.
Better keep those ears a-hearing.
Never know when spook or goblin
from the bushes come a-hobblin'.

Never know when witch a-whooping
from the black sky comes a-swooping.
She'll snatch you far to snake filled den,
never to return again.

Better shudder, better shake.
The explanation that I make
may force from you a curdling scream,
for tonight, tonight is Halloween!

Before Christmas (age 9?)

If you're bad and never good and weep and fuss and cry,
and never gay anytime you play, Santa will pass you by.

But if you're good, as good can be, and do what you are told,
Santa will be good to you and me 'til we're very, very old.

Santa (age 11?)

Santa's packed his bag and sleigh
with lots of candy and toys.
And now he's started on his way
to little girls and boys
to make them glad that they were good
and got all of their wishes
of cars and books and dolly's hood,
and even little fishes.
So go to sleep and don't be blue.
Don't fret, 'cause that's the bunk.
Next year all things you get are new,
and you'll ditch this year's junk.

A Jolly Christmas (age 13)

Christmas is coming, hooray! Hooray!
Christmas will be a beautiful day
with candy and cookies and nuts galore
scattered all up and down the floor.

Christmas is coming, oh what a day!
When children and their pets all play
with brand new toys that shine with might.
They look just like a pretty light.

Christmas is coming, gosh oh gee!
And what a great big Christmas tree
with shining balls of very hue,
a silver star and candles too!

The Little King (age 17)

The star, so brightly shining down up the earth below
had come to rest upon a place that we have learned to know
as being a manger, dry and dark, where on one holy day
a little King to all the world was born amidst the hay.
And as he lay there, quietly, with cow and sheep not far,
three Wise Men, greatest of the world came, guided by the star.
They laid before the little King their gifts of myrrh and gold
and frankincense and many things. And so the story's told
to every child at Christmas time when thoughts go wandering
back to the manger, star and birth of Heaven's Little King.

Mrs Santa's Farewell (age17)

Hey Dasher, Dancer, Prancer and Vixen,
Comet and Cupid, Donner and Blitzen.
Get on your harness and finery too,
You've got to go flying up there in the blue.

For tonight is the night that old Santa and sleigh
load up with toys and get on their way
to every child's house all over the earth,
and make them all happy and filled up with mirth.

And you, little elves, get started to work.
There's plenty to do that tonight you can't shirk.
'Cause everyone's waiting for Santa's gay call,
"Merry Christmas and Happy New Year to All."

So up, up and away you reindeer that fly.
Go faster and faster and glide through the sky.
Leave all your toys and goodies delight
with every good boy and girl in your sight.

And hurry on back with Old Santa and sleigh,
rest up over night and get started next day
to help little elves make new little toys
to take next year to good girls and boys.

The Years (age 14?)

We bring the New Year in with cheers
and smile the old one out.

We're glad the new one's here at last;
the old one will not pout.

The old year's done the very best
we know it ever could.

We know the year approaching
will be better (knock on wood).

So give three cheers, hip, hip, hooray!
For midnight's here at last.

Ahead the future's near to us;
but we'll not forget the past.

DARKER TEEN POEMS

As I was typing this section, I realized this was a very dark period in my life. I was obviously prolific during my seventeenth year, particularly early in the year, but I was pretty depressed. I was waiting to graduate in June so I could finally join the Air Force, and more importantly, get out of my home situation. Since this period I have settled in my mind the questions I had about God. However, I still cannot understand the ways of man or mankind.

The Flight of Time (age 16)

Autumn's the time when leaves grow old and turn from their color green
to red and gold from the coming cold, fall to the ground and begin to mold
'neath the blue of the sky serene.

Next comes Winter with snowy days when the ground turns a glaring white.
On these chilly days inside we stay, as the wind grows fierce along the way,
growling with all its might.

And when in fields the planters sow and insects cease to sleep,
little plants begin to grow, and all around the flowers know,
that Spring is here for keeps.

Then follows Summer, bright and gay when nestlings learn to fly,
and happy children run and play through the meadows all the day
with babbling brooks nearby.

So Autumn's splendor fades and dies, then Winter's hoary rime
gives way to Spring and Summer skies, and season after season flies
until the end of time.

Fate (age 17)

The cold gray walls of the gruesome cell drew nearer, nearer still.
The bars of steel upon the door were there against my will.

The walls were dripping slime upon the filthy floor of stone.
And from my lips each move I made drew forth a stricken moan.

For as the seconds ticked away at each harsh inward breath,
I knew that closer, closer yet upon me crept cold death.

For there with those prison walls each night and day I'd lie
awaiting time to bring along the hour in which I'd die.

The tramp of feet outside my cell told all the time had come.
The dusty clock upon the wall struck out a soundless, one.

The rusted hinges groaned as open wide they threw the gate,
and pulled me up and dragged me out to take me to my fate.

My ragged clothes fell from my limbs to the ground beneath my feet.
The stinking sweat poured from my brow, not from the scorching heat.

Before the wall I stood while thirteen men before me went.
Their eyes were sparks of fire as if from hell to earth were sent.

Their rifles raised, I knew that here upon this very spot,
as thirteen rifles fired as one, I would begin to rot.

I crumpled to the earth, the blood gushed from my bleeding breast.
It would not be too long before I'd have my chance to rest.

And for my deeds upon this earth I knew the penalty well.
My body would stay here in the soil; my soul would burn in Hell.

Destruction (age 17)

The dead lay heaped upon themselves. Soaked with blood was the ground.
The noise was deafening in the air. The shells burst all around.

The cannons roared, the rifles laughed as grenades tore up the earth.
Machine guns rattled through space. To them it all brought mirth.

The human race with its knowledge wide was smart. Oh yes, they knew
just what they did as from hand to hand, from man to man they slew.

Oh yes, they knew how brave they were, for right they fought along.
But who is man that he can say just what is right or wrong?

Who is man that he can kill with the poor excuse of war,
when all he wants is power and wealth. The results? Why he wants more!

For man is never satisfied with what he has in hand.
He still wants more of everything: more air, more sea, more land.

He conquers, steals, and kills for all he thinks he needs to exist.
On battlefield his comrade's found enveloped in a mist.

A mist of death, a life that's spent for nought. No gain in health,
no gain in air or sea or land. No gain in any wealth.

But death, cold, bloody, writhing death for all, for man and beast.
Here and there, north and south, in west and even east.

And man is wise. Oh yes, he knows all that he does quite well.
But still he thinks that Heaven's his, he thinks not of blazing Hell.

Of blazing Hell where life is spent in torture for the past.
He'll burn in fire of charring heat. His damned soul cannot last.

(more)

Yet does he care? And will he cease his everlasting fight?
Oh no! He'll go forever on and never reach a height.

The cannons roared, the rifles laughed, the shells burst overhead.
Machine guns rattled through space. And all around, the dead.

And will man learn before his very existence here on earth
is crushed to dust? Why do you laugh. This should bring no mirth.

For even as you read this now, you know, that as it stands,
man will destroy himself and earth with his own clumsy hands.

Man I (age 17)

The rippling waters, flowing o'er the rocks
unto a wondrous place know as the sea,
all seemed to whisper songs of unknown joys
and future hopes. The birds high in the trees
too sang of sunshine, brilliant light of day.
And all the animals in nature's for'st
were bright and happy. 'Till one moment
there seemed to usher from the Heaven's high
a screeching sound of thunder from the gods.
And all earth trembled 'neath the lightening force.
Then in one tiny garden beautiful
God sent to earth the creature known as man.
Man was sent with great intelligence
and knowledge. Why was he put here upon
this earth if not to better and increase
the beauty? If not to reproduce
and make himself master of all he saw?
Master? Yes! Master of all below him.
But master of the universe? Oh no!
For then he'd overstep his gifted power
of being able to reason and think.
Yet is that not what man wants to do?
To rule the Universe and stars above?
To rule all life, including other men?

Man II (age 17)

Man's hatred for his brother,
his want of power and wealth,
the inevitable blackness of his mind,
will be his end.

He cares for nought but power,
his wants are never few,
the selfishness within his body,
will never mend.

He doesn't care what damage's done,
or whether all's destroyed.
It matters not if blood and soil,
together blend.

The everlasting evil there
within his very heart,
man's wanting, hating evermore,
to death will wend.

'Though he repents, his prayers aren't true,
his every word's a lie.
Finally his even soul,
to hell will send.

Man III (age 17)

Oh yellow moon away above on high.
Upon your throne you see man's every deed.
Why is it stupid man will never heed
your everlasting warnings from the sky.

And do you ever heave a weary sigh
when in his dry fields man plants all his seeds,
and reaps a crop of nought but straggly weeds
while at his side his tools there laying by.

For man is old and weak and pity not
have I for anything he says or does.
His mind, his heart, his even soul is rot.
None but his very self he ever loves.
He'll ne'er exist, his earthly sins will tell,
and send his soul and body straight to hell.

As Time Goes By (age 17)

As flowers, dormant, 'neath the cold ground lie,
the leaves come tumbling down each year at Fall
from gnarled trees, so ancient, stately, tall.
Year follows year the same as time goes by.

And as old Winter fades and Spring grows nigh
the mighty winds blow fierce with cow-like bawl.
Flowers awake, green ivy climbs the wall.
Every year the same as time goes by.

But when it comes to man old nature's rules
are fast forgotten. Man has his own schools.
He lives, he dies, he kills, his fruit he bares.
And it is said by most that well he fares.
But as it is with man, you can't deny,
there's no two years the same as time goes by.

And Came the Spring (age 17)

When old man winter growled around your door.
When snow was high in drifts and days were cold.
Small birds were huddled close in warm down folds,
and all around you'd find old winter's hoar.

Then suddenly the sky broke through once more
and came the spring. And all the world was told
that winter had passed. Came blue skies of old
with warm and sunny days of yesteryore.

And so it is with man. When things go wrong
and all is dark and nought is gay or bright.
When winter's come and birds cease every song.
At once among the gloom you find a light,
and comes the spring. And 'tis not very long
'til once again you find that all is right.

Man IV (age 17)

We are the clay, and God is the Potter. He molds us on the wheel of life
into different shapes and forms. Some beautiful and ornamental, others
useful. He puts us into the oven and bakes us in the fire of Experience.
Then one by one He slowly takes out each article to observe the finished
product. He finds some have faded and lost their beauty, while others
have been greatly enhanced. Some are whole and strong, others chipped
or cracked, and even broken. But the Potter knows He can only become
better by practice; He does not give up. Again and again He lifts the limp,
wet clay in his firm hands and molds it into life, hoping He can better man

Oh Clouds (age17)

Oh you white clouds, what do you see
traveling over land and sea?
Can I imagine in my dreams
the wondrous places that you've seen?

Exotic countries where you've been,
the rolling plains, the leafy glen?
The mountains high and valleys deep?
I only see them in my sleep.

Oh you who are so very free,
not bound in rusty chains like me.
Oh do you realize what's yours
with no long far off foreign shores?

Oh lift me high upon your wings.
Please take me with you to these things.
Don't leave me here to fade away;
to die at the end of each long day.

Why? (age 19)

What is a God? Who, what and why?
I ask but who can tell?
What power has he? What magic charms?
What is the Heaven, Hell?

What right has God to rule the earth
and bring to it such hoar.
Such evil things as hate and greed
and envy, and much more.

Why does he not bring happiness
and peace of mind and soul?
Why can he not bring love to us
to warm the body whole?

Why bloody fields of battles fought?
Why not a peaceful field?
Why cold and lonely, writhing death?
Why not young birth to yield?

Why blazing fire to char to core
destruction all complete?
Why not a brook, a song, a tree,
a quiet village street?

Why not a cloud so snowy white
drifting through soft blue skies?
Why not a song of endless love?
Why must the world breed lies?

Why? Why? Yet who can answer me?
Oh who can tell me why?
No one, I've searched, continue yet
O'er land and sea, through sky.

Oh who in millions after all
can answer questions so?
Where is the one? Oh come to me!
The answers I must know!

AN EPIC POEM

Doings in the Night (age 19)

The warm and gentle breeze was blowing o'er the prairie green.
For many a mile the lowing herd was all that could be seen.

All was serene, they ate of grass and drank of sparkling dew.
While restless clouds were floating on across the endless blue.

The riders tall in saddles worn, endless night and day,
alert kept sharp eyes steadily pealed for a casual stray.

The sun was setting in the west, scarlet filled the sky.
A fire was made for heat and meal, for darkness was close by.

The riders ate and laid to rest as blackness filled the night.
Their dreams were few. The flickering fire cast the only light.

Yet some who watched the herd that night while all the world was still,
were restless as they sat their horses 'top the sloping hill.

Who were these men with eyes of fire, with long and heavy stride?
Carbines sheathed in saddle guards and six-guns at their side?

What filled their minds as all night long they watched the sleeping herd?
Their faces dark, their eyebrows drawn, and not a muscle stirred.

Dressed all in black with two bright six-guns strapped upon his hips,
the leader sat a midnight horse, a snarl upon his lips.

"What fools," thought he, "to let this herd be guarded by such curs.
'Twill soon be mine." He touched his horse with jingling, silver spurs.

(more)

The muscled steed stepped lightly out. The rustlers glanced around.
The swarthy leader gave a nod. From darkness came no sound.

The trail was steep, but horses sure as downward went the band.
A hundred yards from sleeping men, the leader raised his hand.

He gave a sign, three rustlers neared the men upon the ground.
Then back they came, the job was done and all without a sound.

A snickering horse! The leader's head jerked up. What did he hear?
A stumbling, stupid rider bold to ruin his plans so dear?

A bullet sped with whistle shrill close by the leader's ear.
'Twas proof enough they been disclosed, and rider bold was near.

Twelve six-guns blasted straight ahead, then all was silent still.
A lonely wail of coyote drifted down from yonder hill.

* * *

The sun was rising red, the range was cast in weirdest hue.
The sparkling grass was crisp and green, the sky of deepest blue.

The prairie spread from hill to hill, from dale to valley deep.
And rabbits, wild, with cocky ears from hole to hole would leap.

No hoofprints pressed within the dust, no cattle were in sight.
No campfire burned to leave a tale of doings in the night.

Just shadows, deep, of trees, and mist arising with the dawn.
While birds awoke and sun shone down, the gentle breeze blew on.

SONGS

This section is, literally, songs, which means these words are all set to music. However, since I don't play any music, nor have I ever had an appropriate instrument (like a piano) at my disposal along with someone who could write sheet music, the tunes will have to remain with me only, with one exception, my Air Force boot camp graduation song. Yes, I actually wrote two songs in boot camp and taught them to my squadron to sing! Please note all of these songs were written during my seventeenth year and the first three months of my eighteenth year. Meaning they were composed at the same time I was writing the morbid poetry in the previous section and some holiday stuff. Some dichotomy, huh? Also note that at the time of publication, I could still remember the tunes and sing them (as well as I could ever sing!).

My Aching Heart

The moon's not out tonight, where did it go?
The stars won't shine tonight, I'd like to know

why you're not here, within my arms, holding me near?
Why your lips aren't pressed to mine? Please tell me dear.

My dear I love you so. Why must it be
that you will never be here close to me.

I love you still, I always will, 'though we remain apart
Please dear come back to me and still my aching heart.

Hey Mister Moon

Hey, Mister Moon shining bright above us,
    can't you see we're close tonight?

Hey, little stars twinkling there above us,
    always keep us in your sight.

Tonight we're huggin' and kissin',
    we're happy as can be.

There won't be a thing that we're missin'
    as long as she, is here with me.

So Mister Moon won't you kindly stay here
    while she's holding me so tight.

And little stars always light our way here
    each and every lovely night.

For you can see from above us
    I'm cooing like a dove.

Hey Mister Moon shining bright above us,
    can't you see we're both in love.

Choo Choo Train Blues

Oh the choo, choo, choo of the choo choo train
keeps reminding me of the wind and rain,
Of the prairie green, and the sands so dry.
Of the starry night and the blue, blue sky.

Oh the choo, choo, choo of the choo choo train
keeps a-telling me to return again.
But I never should have started to roam,
'cause now I know I'll never go home.

Whooo whooo, listen to that mournful whistle.
Whooo whooo, reminding me of thorn and thistle.
Bringing back again the campfire and its gleaming light.
Bringing back the howling of coyote in the night.

Oh the choo, choo, choo of the choo choo train
keeps a-telling me to return again.
But I never should have started to roam,
'cause now I know I'll never stay home!

Don't Mind the Weather

Don't mind the weather, whether it rains or shines.
Don't mind the weather, darling if you are mine.

The skies are gray when you're away, but I know what to do.
For when your charms are in my arms, the skies will turn to blue.

Don't mind the weather, whether it's dull or bright.
All kinds of weather, still things will turn out right.

So stay right here, be always near, never to part or stray.
Don't mind the weather except when you're away.

Tahitian Night

The night is bright; the sky is blue.
This lovely night was made for two.

The palm trees swaying and the oceans roar.
The hula dancers on a sandy shore.

The moon is there; the stars are high.
Love's everywhere with you and I.

And who could ask for more than the lovely skies,
the night, you, and Tahitian lullabies.

A Trip to Mars

On a trip to Mars in a rocket machine,
Just you and me and our beautiful dream.
We can catch up then on the kisses due,
flying away up there in the blue.

What a thrill it'll be on that trip to Mars.
We can reach right out and pick off the stars.
Never worries or cares as we fly along,
singing this happy song.

And when we land we'll find a place
to build a cottage small.
And then we'll raise a family
of cats and dogs and all.

And we'll be so gay that we'll never roam.
Always stay right there in our little home.
Let's get started dear in a big space car
on that lovely trip to Mars.

WAF of the 43ʳᵈ

We're the WAF (2 beats) of the Forty-Third.
We march along our heads high in the air.
We're the WAF (2 beats) of the Forty-Third.
Where e'er you look you'll find none to compare.

We sing (2 beats) as we march along.
To think we have a gripe is just absurd.
A gig is rarely seen for everything is clean.
We're the WAF of the Forty-Third.

Fox Flight (2 beats) is the very best.
We'll tell you now we're really on the ball.
Fox Flight (2 beats) is the very best.
We work and play and have the time for all.

Our de- (2 beats) tails are always done.
We make the barracks shine without a word.
We sweep and scrub and brush, but we're never in a rush.
We're the WAF of the Forty-Third

43ʳᵈ Graduation Song (tune of Tenderly)

The sun has set, we say goodbye, Forty-Third.
Our hearts are full, we breath a sigh, Forty-Third
We wandered along, you showed us the way.
And now time has come to say:
We'll miss you for we love you so, Forty-Third.
We'd linger on, but we must go, Forty-Third.
Well never forget, so remember this:
you took our love, you kept our hearts, oh Forty-Third.

POEMS AS AN ADULT

From Our Hearts (age 18)

(Given to Sgt Ramona Vilhauer, 3743rd WAF Training Squadron,
Fox Flight 189, Oct 29 to Dec 19, 1951)

We've spent eight week here and now it's time to say so long.
Not goodbye, for somewhere, someday, we'll meet again.

You've captured a piece of each of our hearts, cherish them as
we cherish you.

Remember us, for we'll never forget your help and kindness,
your loyalty and love.

You've taught us the ways of Air Force Life, to help us be the
best of airmen. Our example has been you, and none better could be
found.

So long, but not goodbye.

Seek Ye Joy (age 18?)

Seek ye no joy,
'til you can find it
in the glory of the night,
the wonder of the day,
and the song of the bird.

Love (age 20)

Love is the laughter of a rippling brook
dashing over countless pebbles.

It's the rush of the mighty wind
behind a snowy bank of restless clouds.

Or the rustle of leaves
on a trembling sycamore.

It's the thrill of a robin's song
a'top a lonely hill.

And the tremble of a heart
when footsteps echo.

Love, is you.

Your Letter (age 29)

Your letter, and you, are so close to me
I must put down some small description of my love for you.

I am and have been terribly lonely this past week.
But it is a kind of loneliness
that has come to me seldom,
and never for long.

I am lonely for you, and not for someone, or just anyone.
I think while you are gone I'm discovering new things
to love about you.

And I am only afraid that something apart from the two of us
will keep our love from being realized.

Come home to me. I care that you are all right.

Come home, for you are carrying more of me with you
than just Shemmit.
You have my plans and dreams and thoughts and emotions,
and my love that will not let sleep come.
Thou art bound to cover me.

This may be the only time I will put love on paper
and make written words come alive with passion.

But I will say this one thing more:
I am not sure, but I think I have found an answer
I have looked for, for years, perhaps centuries.

An answer to hunger and unrest.
For even as I am lonely, I am not searching.

Seeking and Finding (age 34)

Within the pale of the moonlit horizon
she waited silently for the sound of a lover.

She breathed with carelessness and consciousness.
Alone, deathly alone.

The sea thundered ravenously
without her ears hearing its sound. Quiet.

Yet she breathed in rushes.
The rushes of the restless and unsatisfied

Wanting to satisfy her caring and self-humiliation
of what she really was and is, today,

She goes alone, not yet to admit what sears her body
and her mind. Reaping the yet unsown

for the harvest of the Autumn. She knows what
will come soon will be for her and her alone.

The anxieties will cease and satisfaction
will be hers, when I am there.

I enter. The bliss and curiosity satisfied;
the sea no longer thunders but now is calm.

White foam brushes the beach and the salt wind scents
her hair. We kiss and the passion of our youth blazes with fire

and flames of wanting. We want and we have.
No longer is she wondering what she is.

For I have told her and made her stop her foolish wondering.
Life is short, but my love will make time non-existent.

We love and we are not alone. We have and need and share,
and never once do we care about the sea and the cold.

Sea Love (age 34)

I lie and listen to the surf breaking ten feet away.
The swish as the waves run up the beach toward my feet,
bubbling foam along the edges.
As the wave returns to the sea it gently sucks everything back,
filtering itself through the sand and pulling at the surface.
An occasional flap of a seagull wing sounds overhead.
The horizon sports a colorful sail here and there.
The sun glistens off white tipped water and waxed surfboards.
Warmth penetrates skin and flesh and bone,
and the fishy-salt smell assaults the nostrils.
This my beloved sea.
May it always bring me peace.

Dreams (age 34)

Consciousness slips away to find you skipping across neurons.
Mentally I reach out, and my fingers encounter the warmth of you beside
me.

Gently my fingers investigate your softness,
my lips supplanting them as they trail to a new discovery.

My loins spring to desire.
My body trembles with need.

But as I open my eyes you disappear in the Venetian-striped sunlight.
All that is left is the desire, the need.

Your image now gently caresses memory patterns.
Is the dream of you all I shall ever have again?

Sea Love II (age 34)

Sea: green, olive in the morning sunlight.
Calm swells white tipped by the breeze. But fickle.
Calm most of the time, but occasionally tossing a tantrum of spray
in your face.
Odiferous with kelp, fish, mollusks – hello little starfish –
and people.

Tide: unable to make up its mind to come or go.
Cutting a bank in the sand one second only to quickly erase it in
the next.

Wind: cold, out of the north, tingling along the spine without heed
of a trillion layers of cloth or 98.6 degrees.

Sun: haloed at a misty hour, weaving a path across the ocean surface,
it's reflection bandied about by endless swells.

Clouds: stratus layers below the sun, unaffected by the breeze,
maintaining their stability 'til they eventually disintegrate.

Seagulls: feeding casually in the icy water and soaring effortlessly on
the breeze.
Playing hopscotch with the surf and catch-as-catch-can with sand crabs.
White, brown, speckled – and lonely.

Jets: echoing overhead, a thousand people escaping to a dream.
Or a nightmare.

People: only fools like me on a beach at eight on a December morning.
Modalities mingle to exquisite pleasure. Peace.
Yet I am not quite alone. Others too are here, escaping, dreaming, dying.
Or maybe like me, they're holding love tightly to their hearts.

Goodbyes (age 40+)

After a while you learn the subtle difference
between holding a hand, and chaining a soul.

You learn love doesn't mean leaning,
and company doesn't always mean security.

You begin to learn that kisses aren't contracts
and presents aren't promises.

You accept defeats with the grace of an adult,
not the grief of a child.

You learn to build all your roads on today
because tomorrow's ground is too unstable for plans,

and futures have a way of falling down in mid-flight.
Eventually you learn even sunshine burns if you have too much.

So plant your own garden and toil your own soil
instead of waiting for someone to bring you flowers.

You learn you really can endure, you really are strong,
and you really do have worth.

You learn something new
with every goodbye.

Love II (about age 60)

Love is warm,
like the summer sun resting on your back.

Love is gentle,
like an autumn breeze rustling the leaves.

Love crackles,
like the fire on the hearth in the cold of winter.

Love renews itself,
like a bud bursting into a flower in Spring.

And even in parting,
love remains in the heart – forever.